Contents

D1286603

A Cognitive Workout

The fountain of youth exists only in folklore and fairy tales, but that hasn't stopped professionals, laypeople, and everyone in between from attempting to uncover the secrets behind good health and longevity. We all want to stay young and active in order to lead fulfilling lives, but to achieve this, we have to keep our bodies *and* our minds in top shape. How do we do this? Well, there is plenty of information regarding the care of our bodies, but relatively little attention has been paid to the importance of taking care of our minds. That's why this publication is so valuable. *Brain Games™: Ultimate Brain Booster Puzzles* is an excellent resource that will help you keep your brain fit for life.

The human brain thrives on learning and experiencing new things—it is stimulated by both novelty and challenge. If something is routine or too easy, our brains are essentially operating on autopilot—which doesn't require a lot of mental attention and does little to boost cerebral strength. By exposing ourselves to new activities and information, we are exercising our brains in a way that will keep them sharp and focused.

To maintain cognitive fitness, you have to get your head in the game (pun intended). "Use it or lose it!" should be your motto from now on, and working the puzzles in this publication is a great way to put those words into action so you can start to benefit from them.

Researchers use the term "cognitive reserve" to explain the importance of

Ultimate Brain Booster Puzzles

Consultant: Elkhonon Goldberg, Ph.D.

Publications International, Ltd.

Elkhonon Goldberg, Ph.D., ABPP/ABCN (consultant) is a clinical professor of neurology at New York University School of Medicine, a diplomate of the American Board of Professional Psychology/ American Board of Clinical Neuropsychology, and director of The East-West Science and Education Foundation. Dr. Goldberg created the Manhattan-based Cognitive Enhancement Program, a fitness center for the brain, and is author of the international best-selling books *The Wisdom Paradox: How Your Mind Can Grow as Your Brain Grows Older* and *The Executive Brain: Frontal Lobes and the Civilized Mind.*

Puzzle Constructors: Michael Adams, Cihan Altay, Myles Callum, Philip Carter, Kelly Clark, Barry Clarke, Conceptis Puzzles, Don Cook, Jeanette Dall, Mark Danna, Harvey Estes, Josie Falkner, Adrian Fisher, Holli Fort, Erich Friedman, Ray Hamel, Luke Haward, Dick Hess, Marilynn Huret, Dan Meinking, Kate Mepham, Patrick Merrell, David Millar, Dan Moore, Michael Moreci, Alan Olschwang, Ellen F. Pill, Ph.D., Dave Roberts, Marylin Roberts, Stephen Ryder, Gianni Sarcone, Pete Sarjeant, Stephen Schaefer, Paul Seaburn, Fraser Simpson, Terry Stickels, Howard Tomlinson

Illustrators: Cihan Altay, Hyelim An, Elizabeth Gerber, Nicole H. Lee, Dave Roberts, Marylin Roberts, Jay Soto, Shavan R. Spears

Consultant: Julie K. Cohen

Brain Games is a trademark of Publications International, Ltd.

ISBN-13: 978-1-60553-300-1
ISBN-10: 1-60553-300-9

Manufactured in China.

8 7 6 5 4 3 2 1

building brain power from an early age. In doing so, you are creating a "cushion" that will keep your brain in good operating order as you get older. But it's never too late to start working on brain fitness. "Now" is the best time to learn to play a musical instrument, to enroll in a new class—and to take advantage of all this publication has to offer.

Take a few minutes to familiarize yourself with the wide variety of puzzles in this book (as well as their levels of difficulty). Different kinds of puzzles stimulate different parts of the brain, and you should exercise as many of those areas as possible. To help you choose the puzzles that will provide the most benefit, we've labeled each one with the cognitive functions it exercises (computation, language, logic, and memory are just a few). Consider doing a variety of puzzles each day so that you don't limit the scope of your workout. Like physical fitness, cognitive fitness can be the result of consistently challenging—and varied—workouts.

Finally, don't forget that puzzles are a lot of fun to solve—think of the simple enjoyment you derive from working a crossword or finding your way through a twisting maze. The pleasure of sitting back and doing a puzzle is not only relaxing—it can also help relieve stress after a long day. Another great thing about this publication is that it's small enough to carry anywhere: to the park, the doctor's office, or on a trip out of town. Whenever you have a chance, turn your downtime into brain-boosting time—and think of the fun you'll have while doing it!

PLANNING

CREATIVE THINKING

Vex-a-Gon

Place the numbers 1 through 6 into the triangles of each hexagon. The numbers may be in any order, but they do not repeat within each hexagon shape.

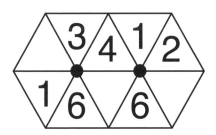

LANGUAGE   PLANNING

Word Columns

Find the hidden phrase by using the letters directly above each of the blank squares. Each letter is used only once. A black square indicates the end of a word.

	y				u	a	n		w		r	e		s			a	t		
o	h	s			h	l	l		h	a	m	i		i		o	w	l		
a	h	i	a	j	o	w	r	o	w	o	t	h	a	g	s	o	u	n	w
T	f	e	s	f	e	s	t	d	c	o	m	e	n	t	t	o	r	e	s
			■						■							■			
■						■								■					■
			■					■							■				
		■										■						■	

Answers on page 246.

A Puzzling Perspective

Mentally arrange the lettered balls from large to small in the correct order to spell an 11-letter word.

Clue: A type of clock

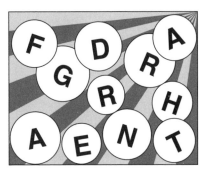

Liar's Logic

Use the following information to figure out who is lying and who is telling the truth. There are 2 truth-tellers and 1 liar.

Person A says person B is lying.

Person B says person A is lying.

Person C says person A is telling the truth.

Answers on page 246.

The Great Ape Hunt

Track down each of these "King Kong"–related terms in the group of letters on the next page. Words may be found horizontally, vertically, or diagonally. They may read forward or backward. Leftover letters reveal an interesting bit of trivia about this classic 1933 movie.

ANIMATRONICS

ANN DARROW

BROADWAY

BRUCE CABOT

CARL DENHAM

EMPIRE STATE

FAY WRAY

GORILLA

JACK DRISCOLL

JUNGLE

NEW YORK

PANIC

RKO

ROBERT ARMSTRONG

SKULL ISLAND

SPECIAL EFFECTS

STOP MOTION

VENTURE

```
G S T C E F F E L A I C E P S
A N J A C K D R I S C O L L T
S L O T E Y A W D A O R B T O
C Y A R W Y A F R N A T E O P
I T I T T L E S F O R T H B M
N D N A L S I L L U K S E A O
O M E O V I M E W E R E T C T
R H W E M P I R E S T A T E I
T E Y E I G K P A R H T G C O
A H O W O O N D A T U O E U N
M R R J U N G L E N R T T R H
I E K A P E K I N I I E N B G
N A M A H N E D L R A C B E P
A E T H E B E L A S T A N O V
D K W O R R A D N N A O N G R
```

Leftover letters spell: _____

_____

☼ Trivia on the Brain

People continue to debate what they consider to
be the most difficult puzzle. But they will likely
never agree, because a puzzle that is difficult for
one person may be easy for another.

SPATIAL REASONING

World's Easiest Crossword

You can solve this crossword in record time, because we've removed the clues and turned it into a maze, instead. Start at top left.

PLANNING

LANGUAGE

Say What?

Below are a group of words that, when properly arranged in the blanks, reveal a quote from Booker T. Washington.

living   thing   up   man   lifting   only   fellow   is

"The _____ _____ worth _____ for _____ the _____

_____ of our _____ _____."

CREATIVE THINKING

10

Answers on page 246.

Sudoku

Use deductive logic to complete the grid so that each row, each column, and each 3 by 3 box contains the numbers 1 through 9 in some order. The solution is unique.

2					1			8
	3	8						6
		6			9		5	
	9	7			8			2
		1	7	2	3	5		
5			9			8	7	
	8		1			7		
9						1	8	
3			4					9

⚙ Trivia on the Brain

There are approximately 100 billion neurons in the human brain, which allow information to travel at speeds up to 268 miles per hour.

Answer on page 246.

Between the Lines

Solve for the middle (undefined) word in each 3-word set. For each set, all 3 words appear on the same page in the dictionary in the order they are given. Rearrange the middle words to reveal a quote from Euripedes.

Example: putter: to work at random; tinker
        puzzle
        pygmy: one of a race of dwarfs

_ _ _ _ _ m: the quality of having experience,
        knowledge, and good judgment

_ _ _ _
_ _ s h: feel a strong desire or hope for something

d _ _ _ _ _: to administer, manage, supervise
_ _ _ _ _ _ _ o n
_ _ _ _ _ _ _ o r: one of a group of people who govern
        the affairs of a company

_ _ _ f t: the act of stealing
_ _ _ _ r
_ _ _ _: the objective case of "they"

f _ _ _: of, or originating from, the common people
_ _ _ _ _ w
_ _ _ _ _: a foolish action, practice, or idea; absurdity

"The _____(st) men _____ _____ own _____."

Answers on page 246.

Quic-Kross

This is a crossword puzzle with a twist. Use the clues to solve the puzzle. When complete, the circled letters will spell out a "mystery word."

Across

1. Kettle
2. Feed (past tense)
3. Disobedient

Down

4. Symbolic or aesthetic expression
5. Small, industrious insect
6. Flying mammal

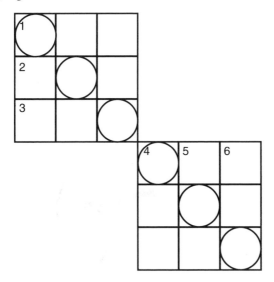

Mystery word hint: Undue emphasis on book learning

Alien Mutations

Shown are 9 mutation chambers surrounded by alien figures. Each of the 3 aliens on the left passed through the 3 chambers to the right and was transformed on the other side (e.g., the alien on the left of A passed through chambers A, B, and C and mutated into the alien on the right of C). The same is true for the aliens above the chambers: Each passed through the 3 chambers directly below them and came out mutated on the other side.

Each chamber effects one—and only one—alteration (changes in head or body shape, changes in posture, adding/removing appendages).

What mutation is each chamber responsible for?

Answers on page 247.

Cross-Math

Place the digits 1 through 9 in the empty white squares so that the 3 horizontal and 3 vertical equations are true. Each digit will be used exactly once. Calculations are done from left to right and from top to bottom.

	-		÷		=	1
+		+		×		
	×		-		=	66
÷		×		-		
	-		-		=	2
=		=		=		
2		10		14		

Wacky Wordy

Can you "read" the phrase below?

L O V E A A L L I S F A I R N D W A R

The Loopy Lexicon

You probably won't find the clues for these 10 words in your typical dictionary. But they're a fun way of looking at words in a fresh and "logical" way. Or is that "psycho"-logical?

Across

1. Insect that lives on castaways?
4. Boat just for guys?
7. Thug with a babe?
8. Wacky way to move?
9. Light rain in Italy?
10. Baby talk?

Down

2. Unisex wedding attendant?
3. Less hairy race?
5. Dance tunes for lumberjacks?
6. Prison seminar?

The words:

BALDERDASH
FELLOWSHIP
BIGAMIST
LITTERBUG
BRIDEGROOM
LOCOMOTION
CONCOURSE
LOGARITHMS
FATHERHOOD
PREDICTION

Answer on page 247.

ATTENTION
VISUAL SEARCH
ANALYSIS

Find the Word

Ignoring spaces, capitalization, and punctuation, find all 19 occurrences of the consecutive letters L-O-V-E in this paragraph.

Clover loved working at the glove factory, but her dream was to start a solo venture making rollover bars and covers for convertibles. For lunch, she ate buffalo, vegetables, and cheese cooked in a small oven. Her lunch occasionally had spillover, so she cleaned the small oven with Brillo very carefully. Clover's boyfriend, Glover, who worked at the coverall factory, loved the freckles she had all over her face. The two lovebirds dated often but never had sleepovers. Glover longed to be a portobello vendor but instead went to night school to study piccolo, ventilator repair, and pullover design.

Name Calling

Decipher the encoded words in the quip below using the numbers and letters on the phone pad. Each number can stand for 3 or 4 possible letters.

If you can't 2–4–8–3, don't 7–4–6–9 your 8–3–3–8–4.

1	2 ABC	3 DEF
4 GHI	5 JKL	6 MNO
7 PQRS	8 TUV	9 WXYZ
	0	

VISUAL LOGIC

SPATIAL VISUALIZATION

CREATIVE THINKING

Oddball of the Group

Which figure is the odd one out?

A.

B.

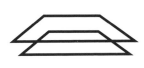

C.

D.

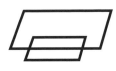

E.

F.

Trivia on the Brain

Fevers are controlled by the part of the brain called the hypothalamus. The highest body temperature ever recorded is 115 degrees F. Temperatures greater than 109 degrees can be fatal.

Answer on page 248.

Sudoku

Use deductive logic to complete the grid so that each row, each column, and each 3 by 3 box contains the numbers 1 through 9 in some order. The solution is unique.

8	2				6			
1	5	7						9
		9						8
6	8	1	5		7		9	4
	9		1		4		8	
3	4		9		8	1	7	6
5						8		
2				6			1	3
		4					6	2

Arrow Web

Shade in some of the arrows so that each arrow in the grid points to exactly 1 shaded arrow.

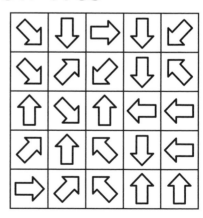

Answers on page 248. **19**

Use Some Sense

Across

1. Continuous movement
5. Dog that spotted Peter Pan
9. Revival technique
12. "No sweat"
13. Run amok
14. Arles assent
15. Be suspicious
17. Orderly supervisors: abbr.
18. Shopaholic's activity
19. Court shout
21. Do some work on a dairy farm
24. Kind of test
25. Mischievous sort
28. Without restraint
32. Sport without tackling
35. 1982 NCAA basketball champs
36. The heavens
37. Corn spike
38. Hard-to-break hold
41. Become furious
44. Otherworldly
48. Dernier ___ (latest thing)
49. Food sampling
52. Coffee container
53. "Aha!"
54. Chieftain's charge
55. Chinese restaurant syndrome substance
56. Chew the fat
57. Georgetown athlete

Down

1. Parker who played Crockett
2. Light fixture
3. Computer customer
4. Tree tissue
5. Pistol-packing PAC
6. Ventilate
7. Dad on the ark
8. Stab, of sorts
9. Bullfight arenas
10. Shrimpish
11. Court order?
16. Floral neckpiece
20. Sheik's subject

22. Longest prison sentence
23. Hillock
25. Cousin on "The Addams Family"
26. Extinct flightless bird
27. Turning to mush
29. Not great
30. Certain lodge member
31. Stallone nickname
33. Cook too hot
34. Religious dissenter

39. Bee follower
40. Two-master
41. Riffraff
42. Miscalculates
43. Fast race
45. Move, in real estate lingo
46. Holmesian exclamation
47. Active European volcano
50. Dead ___ Scrolls
51. Vietnamese celebration

PLANNING

CREATIVE THINKING

Vex-a-Gon

Place the numbers 1 through 6 into the triangles of each hexagon. The numbers may be in any order, but they do not repeat within each hexagon shape.

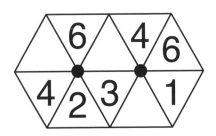

LOGIC

LANGUAGE

Learned Crypto-quote

Cryptograms are messages in substitution code. Break the code to reveal the quote and its author. For example, THE SMART CAT might become FVO QWGDF JGF if **F** is substituted for **T, V** for **H, O** for **E,** and so on.

"A'QC GCQCV KCB XJ

LOIMMKAGE AGBCVSCVC UABI

XJ CRPODBAMG." —XDVN BUDAG

Answers on page 248.

You Are Here

…and the taxi meter is ticking. This professional building is a maze of corridors and cubicles. Elevators are available, but there are no stairs. And overstressed office workers won't give you directions to the exit. Why, oh why, did you ever come in here? Doesn't matter now—time to get moving!

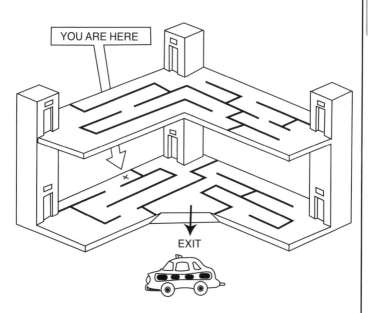

PLANNING

LANGUAGE

Word Ladder

Use the clues to change just one letter on each line to go from the top word to the bottom word. Do not change the order of the letters. You must have a common English word at each step.

GONE

_____ give it to a dog

_____ something irksome

_____ essentials

_____ farmyard building

BORN

COMPUTATION

ANALYSIS

Number Crossword

Fill in this crossword with numbers instead of letters. Use the clues to determine which number from 1 through 9 belongs in each empty square. No zeros are used.

Across
1. A multiple of 9
3. Consecutive digits, ascending
6. Consecutive digits, ascending
7. A multiple of 11

Down
1. A palindrome
2. Three different digits
4. Three different digits
5. Consecutive even digits, ascending

Answers on page 248.

Rhyme Time

Each clue leads to a 2-word answer that rhymes, such as BIG PIG or STABLE TABLE. The numbers in parentheses after the clue give the number of letters in each word.

1. Order from the boss (3, 2): _____

2. Police chief (3, 3): _____

3. Poor hitter's aid (3, 3): _____

4. Dinner call (4, 3): _____

5. Previous year's performers (4, 4): _____

6. Small horse's pal (4, 5): _____

7. Despots on the red planet (4, 5): _____

8. Another left flip-flop (5, 5): _____

9. Candy with fresh-brewed flavor (6, 6): _____

10. Parts of news shows (6, 7): _____

Trivia on the Brain

The brain of a grasshopper has approximately 16,000 neurons. The human brain contains 100 billion neurons.

Answers on page 249.

PLANNING

LANGUAGE

Word Columns

Find the hidden quote by using the letters directly above each of the blank squares. Each letter is used only once. A black square indicates the end of a word.

i		g	e		c	i	w		k	t			c		k			o		
s	e	e	e	c	i	w	a		k	i	l		l	o	o	s		i	n	d
L	t	d	i	h	f	t	a	t	l	e	s	d	e	a	h	e	a	v	t	f
o	o	s	o		o	s		o	s		d	e		e	a	e	f	t		t

LOGIC

CREATIVE THINKING

Figure This Out in Your Own Good Time

Where is 17 sometimes 5 and 11 sometimes 23?

Answers on page 249.

Hashi

Each circle represents an island, with the number inside indicating the number of bridges connected to it. Draw bridges between islands using the number given, but there can be no more than 2 bridges going in the same direction, and there must be a continuous path connecting all islands. Bridges can be only vertical or horizontal and may not cross islands or other bridges. We've drawn some bridges to get you started.

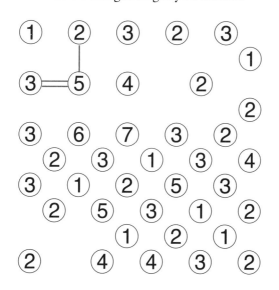

VISUAL SEARCH

ATTENTION

It's a Small Word, After All

The words below are contained within the group of letters to the right. They can be found horizontally, vertically, or diagonally and read backward or forward.

AM	HE	OR
AN	HO	OX
AS	IF	OY
AT	IN	RE
BE	IT	TE
BY	LA	TO
DO	MA	UH
FA	ME	YO
GO	NO	
HA	OH	

```
Y  N  A  H
O  N  A  O
M  Y  R  H
S  A  U  H
A  H  O  E
M  T  B  F
L  A  G  A
M  O  O  N
E  T  I  F
R  I  D  I
E  E  T  O
B  Y  H  X
```

Answer on page 249.

Say What?

Below are a group of words that, when properly arranged in the blanks, reveal a quote from George Orwell.

joke   mental   a   dirty   rebellion

"A _____ _____ is _____ sort of _____ _____."

Fitting Words

In this miniature crossword, the clues are listed randomly and are numbered for convenience only. It is up to you to figure out the placement of the 9 answers. To help you, we've inserted one letter (an **I**) in the grid, and this is the only occurrence of that letter in the completed puzzle.

Clues
1. Capital of France
2. Member of a cast
3. Learning method
4. _____ and carrots
5. Vassal
6. Ledge
7. Curved part of the foot
8. Wear away
9. False god

LOGIC

LANGUAGE

Crypto-group: European Cities

Cryptograms are messages in substitution code. Break the code to reveal 5 European cities. For example, THE SMART CAT might become FVO QWGDF JGF if **F** is substituted for **T, V** for **H, O** for **E,** and so on.

K N O T

P M K R M K

S E A O T P M K E

Q T K N O T

S T A P N K

SPATIAL VISUALIZATION

A Puzzling Perspective

Mentally arrange the lettered balls from large to small in the correct order to spell an 11-letter word.

Clue: With certainty

LANGUAGE

30

Answers on page 249.

Level 1

Girls' Names Letterbox

The letters in the name ZOE can be found in boxes 4, 17, and 19, but not necessarily in that order. The same is true for the other names listed below. Using the names and the box numbers that follow each name as your guide, insert all the letters of the alphabet into the boxes. If you do this correctly, the shaded cells will reveal another name.

Hint: Look for words that share a single letter. For example, KATE shares only an **A** with LAURA and only an **E** with QUEENIE. By comparing the number lists following the names, you can deduce the box numbers of the shared letters.

BETH: 5, 7, 17, 25

BRENDA: 5, 15, 17, 18, 20, 23

CILLA: 21, 22, 23, 24

DAVINA: 15, 16, 20, 21, 23

FRANCES: 6, 10, 17, 18, 20, 22, 23

GLADYS: 6, 12, 14, 15, 23, 24

JOSIE: 1, 6, 17, 19, 21

KATE: 3, 17, 23, 25

LAURA: 13, 18, 23, 24

MARY: 14, 18, 23, 26

MAXINE: 2, 17, 20, 21, 23, 26

PATSY: 6, 11, 14, 23, 25

QUEENIE: 8, 13, 17, 20, 21

WANDA: 9, 15, 20, 23

ZOE: 4, 17, 19

1	2	3	4	5	6	7	8	9	10	11	12	13

14	15	16	17	18	19	20	21	22	23	24	25	26

Answers on page 249. **31**

LANGUAGE

GENERAL KNOWLEDGE

Time for a Rhyme

The name of the game for this puzzle is easy-breezy. To solve the clues, find an apt rhyming phrase from the list supplied (there are more choices than you'll need). For instance, if the clue were "focused on the goal," you'd probably guess the rhyming phrase to be "eyes on the prize." We've filled in a few squares to get you started.

Across

8. Golden oldie
9. Vacation at the beach
10. Chill; not make a fuss

Down

1. Have a spree at the mall
2. Restless
3. Kind of auto transmission
4. The big boss
5. Any means possible
6. Real fast
7. Spy satellite

The choices:

Best of the west
Eye in the sky
Blast from the past
Built to the hilt
Ants in the pants
Set it and forget it
Go with the flow
Cruisin' for a bruisin'
Shop till you drop
Large and in charge
Dare to compare
Pedal to the metal
Hook or by crook
Made in the shade
Four on the floor
Fun in the sun

Twenty-four Jumble

Arrange the numbers and math signs in this cornucopia to come up with the number 24.

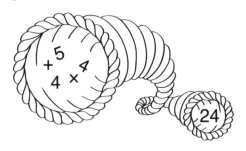

ANALYSIS   COMPUTATION

Fish Fantasy

This tank is just swimming with fish. Can you find the two that match?

Answer on page 250.

Word Ladder

Use the clues to change just one letter on each line to go
from the top word to the bottom word. Do not change
the order of the letters. You must have a common
English word at each step.

LOAN

_____ of bread

_____ take one from my book

_____ slender

_____ a seed

_____ tired

PEAT

Orderly Sequence

What letter is missing?

Z, ___, T, T, F, F, S, S, E, N

1-2-3

Place the numbers 1, 2, and 3 in the circles below. The challenge is to have only these 3 numbers in each connected row and column—no number should repeat. Any combination is allowed.

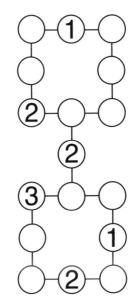

 Trivia on the Brain

An average 6-year-old understands approximately 13,000 words; high school graduates know at least 60,000 words.

Answer on page 250.

Wacky Wordy

Can you "read" the phrase below?

HASTE - H + W = WASTE

Sudoku

Use deductive logic to complete the grid so that each row, each column, and each 3 by 3 box contains the numbers 1 through 9 in some order. The solution is unique.

1	2			7		5	6	
5		7	9	3	2		8	
					1			
	1		2	4			5	
3		8				4		2
	7			8	5		1	
			7					
	8		4	2	3	7		1
	3	4		1			2	8

Around the House

This house-shape crossword is filled with—guess what?—stuff you would find around the house. Because the letters don't intersect as in a conventional crossword, we've placed some letters in the house to help you solve the puzzle.

Across
4. It's found around the house
6. Night spot
7. All, for one
10. Sitters
12. Aladdin's vehicle
15. It usually gets a good talking to
16. Stills, maybe
17. Singer's asset

Down
1. Hot spot
2. It does Windows (more often than not)
3. Tool-belt item
5. Type of tumbler
7. Pupil's place
8. Ernie Kovacs called it "a medium because it is neither rare nor well done"
9. Another word for "house"
11. Spillane's private eye
12. _____ potato
13. It's often found under a nut
14. Bibliophile's collection

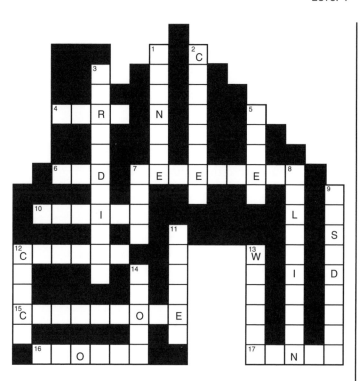

At the Zoo

Every word listed is contained within the group of letters below. Words can be found in a straight line horizontally, vertically, or diagonally. They can be read either backward or forward.

BEAR	HIPPOPOTAMUS	PANTHER
EAGLE	HYENA	PENGUIN
ELEPHANT	LION	RHINOCEROS
GAZELLE	LYNX	SNAKE
GIRAFFE	MACAW	TIGER
GNU	MONKEY	WOLF
GORILLA	PANDA	

```
R  A  E  B  Z  G  A  Z  E  L  L  E  G
E  G  S  O  R  E  C  O  N  I  H  R  O
H  I  P  P  O  P  O  T  A  M  U  S  R
T  R  L  A  J  X  E  A  O  E  U  N  I
N  A  I  W  N  A  N  N  N  A  A  L
A  F  O  O  G  D  K  Y  G  E  N  K  L
P  F  N  L  T  E  A  T  L  U  Y  E  A
E  E  E  F  Y  W  A  C  A  M  I  H  D
R  E  G  I  T  E  L  E  P  H  A  N  T
```

Answer on page 250.

ABCD Numbered

Every cell in this 6 by 6 grid contains 1 of the following 4 letters: A, B, C, or D. No letter can be horizontally or vertically adjacent to itself. The tables above and to the left of the grid indicate how many times each letter appears in that column or row. Can you complete the grid?

				A	0	3	0	3	0	3
				B	0	2	1	2	1	3
				C	3	1	2	1	2	0
A	B	C	D	3	0	3	0	3	0
0	3	0	3						
3	0	3	0						
0	2	2	2						
3	1	1	1						
0	3	2	1						
3	0	1	2						

Annual Sequence

Identify the pair of missing letters.

NR DR ____ FY MH AL MY JE

Word Jigsaw

Fit the pieces into the frame to form common, uncapitalized words reading across and down. There's no need to rotate the pieces; they'll fit as shown, with each piece used exactly once.

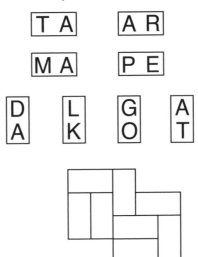

Trivia on the Brain

The Greek philosopher Aristotle believed that the heart, not the brain, was the seat of mental processes. Most people at the time agreed, which is where the term "memorize by heart" comes from.

Answer on page 251.

Shall We Dance?

Have you ever heard of the allemande, the Bihu dance of India, or the chacarrera of Argentina? Neither had we until we looked at this puzzle. Fortunately, we haven't included any of those exotic steps—but we think you'll know these dances. Decipher the anagrams and match them to the pictures below.

1. FLANK COED

2. DECAL BY LEN

3. EARNED BACK

4. SQUANDER ACE

5. CALF OMEN

6. CADET NAP

A.

B.

C.

D.

E.

F.

Answers on page 251. 43

LOGIC
ANALYSIS

The Yellow-Brick Road

The yellow-brick road splits into the green- and the red-brick roads, which lead (respectively) to the red city, which is full of only truth-tellers; and the green city, which is full of only liars. Once I've traveled on either the red or green road, I can't travel back along it. But there is another route between the cities—a blue-brick road. I can't find it without the advice of locals, and I can ask only one resident of each city one question: If I want to visit both cities, which road should I go down first?

A. The red road

C. Either road will do

B. The green road

D. I can't visit both cities

LOGIC

Sudoku

Use deductive logic to complete the grid so that each row, each column, and each 3 by 3 box contains the numbers 1 through 9 in some order. The solution is unique.

	5			6			7	8
				8			5	3
		3	1		4	2		
1	2	5	7				9	
4			8		5			2
	8				2	5	1	6
		2	9		1	3		
5	3			2				
7	9			4			2	

Answers on page 251.

Uncrossed Paths

Draw lines to like symbols (triangle to triangle, star to star) without any line crossing another line. A black line cannot be crossed, and a striped line can be crossed only once.

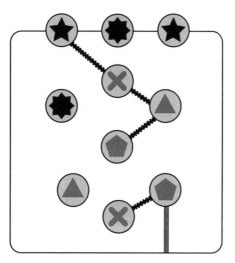

 Trivia on the Brain

Located in the lower back portion of the brain, the cerebellum ("little brain") controls such things as posture, walking, and coordination. Scientists also think the cerebellum plays a role in the way scents are processed.

ANALYSIS

Name Calling

Decipher the encoded words in the quip below using the numbers and letters on the phone pad. Each number can stand for 3 or 4 possible letters.

1	2 ABC	3 DEF
4 GHI	5 JKL	6 MNO
7 PQRS	8 TUV	9 WXYZ
	0	

Make sure to be in with your 3–7–8–2–5–7 if you're going to fall out with your 7–8–7–3–7–4–6–7–7.

PLANNING

LANGUAGE

Word Ladder

Use the clues to change just one letter on each line to go from the top word to the bottom word. Do not change the order of the letters. You must have a common English word at each step.

> PORCH
>
> _____ small bag
>
> _____ comfy seating for a few
>
> _____ to clear the throat
>
> _____ not smooth
>
> ROUGE

Answers on page 251.

Hashi

Each circle represents an island, with the number inside indicating the number of bridges connected to it. Draw bridges between islands using the number given, but there can be no more than 2 bridges going in the same direction, and there must be a continuous path connecting all islands. Bridges can be only vertical or horizontal and may not cross islands or other bridges. We've drawn some bridges to get you started.

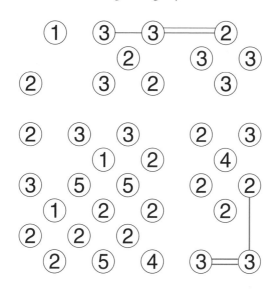

LOGIC

Movie Mania

A movie enthusiast plans to go to the cinema and has decided on his preferences, but he has copied them into his diary incorrectly. Although each item is in the correct column, only one item in each column is positioned correctly. The following facts are true about the correct order:

1. Screenz is not second.

2. Owen McAllen is 1 place above Olympic.

3. Neither Tim Panks nor Owen McAllen are first.

4. Screenz is 1 place below Gladys Hater.

5. Neither Lord Sings nor Gladys Hater are third.

Can you give the movie, the cinema, and the star for each position?

	Movie	Cinema	Star
1	Gladys Hater	Screenz	Ross Crawe
2	Forest Chump	Premiere	Tim Panks
3	Lord Sings	Worldwide	Owen McAllen
4	Atlantic 11	Olympic	Bud Pott

Answers on page 252.

It's a Big Block

My house is ninth from one end of the row and third from
the other end. How many houses are there in the row?

A Puzzling Perspective

Mentally arrange the lettered balls from large to small in
the correct order to spell an 11-letter word.

Clue: Not required

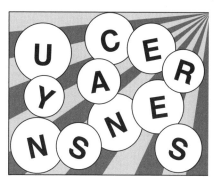

COMPUTATION

ANALYSIS

Don't Miss the Boat On This One

Study these numbers carefully.

3 7 8 2

1 2 6 3 4 4

9 7 4

5 3 7 5

2 1 2 2 3 4 3 3

7 1 1 3 4 2 2

Based on your observation, which number is missing from this sequence?

3 3 5 5 _ 2 1

LANGUAGE

Anagram Heroes

Below are anagrams of 4 famous people. Which is NOT an anagram of a well-known Hollywood director?

A LEWD LOONY

CAROUSEL EGG

GREBE PINT VESSEL

SHADIEST MOON

Answers on page 252.

Cube Count

How many individual cubes are in this configuration? Assume all rows and columns are complete unless you see them end.

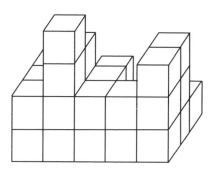

Say What?

Below are a group of words that, when properly arranged in the blanks, reveal a quote from Aristotle.

adversity   and   ornament   prosperity   refuge

"Education is an _____ in _____ _____

a _____ in _____."

ATTENTION | VISUAL SEARCH

Family Circle

All the words listed here are contained in the group of letters. The words can be found in a straight line horizontally, vertically, or diagonally. They can be read either forward or backward. When you have circled all the words, the remaining letters spell 3 more family-related terms.

ANCESTOR   NIECE   SON

AUNT   SIBLING   UNCLE

BROTHER   SISTER   WIFE

CHILD

COUSIN

DAUGHTER

FATHER

GRANDMA

GRANDPA

HOUSEHOLD

HUSBAND

KINFOLK

MOTHER

NEPHEW

```
M A K I N F O L K E A
R R I A G G A E R F M
D H O W R R G T E I D
D O Y R A D N C H W N
A U U O N N I L T E A
U S D T D A L T O H R
G E L S P B B U M P G
H H I E A S I S T E R
T O H C O U S I N N R
E L C N U H N I E C E
R D E A B R O T H E R
```

Leftover letters spell: _____

_____

52   *Answers on page 252.*

Quic-Kross

This is a crossword puzzle with a twist. Use the clues to solve the puzzle. When complete, the circled letters will spell out a "mystery word."

Across
1. Relaxation
2. Large black-and-white mammal
3. Final
4. After expected time

Down
5. Cost per unit
6. On top of
7. Slow leak
8. Expired

Mystery word hint: Quiet, conservative

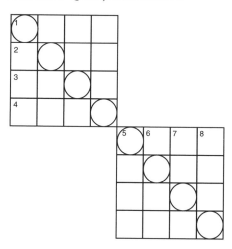

Relations Problem

A man points to a woman and says, "That woman's mother-in-law and my mother-in-law are mother and daughter—in some order." In what ways can the woman be related to the man?

Answers on pages 252–253. **53**

Hat's Off

Can you find the 12 differences between the windows of this stylish hat shop?

Answers on page 253.

Calcu-doku

Use arithmetic and deductive logic to complete the grid so that each row and each column contains the numbers 1 through 4 in some order. Numbers in each outlined set of squares combine to produce the number in the top corner using the mathematical sign indicated.

2/	4×	3×	
		3+	1-
18×			
		6+	

Word Ladder

Use the clues to change just one letter on each line to go from the top word to the bottom word. Do not change the order of the letters. You must have a common English word at each step.

BATTER

_____ witty exchange

_____ to haggle

_____ holds up a stocking

_____ to gather

_____ person who makes silly faces

BURNER

Vex-a-Gon

Place the numbers 1 through 6 into the triangles of each hexagon. The numbers may be in any order, but they do not repeat within each hexagon shape.

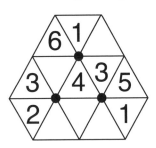

Made in the USA

These clues will help you fill the grid on the next page with 10 items of Americana. The numbers in parentheses indicate the number of letters in each word of the answer.

Across

2. Cody, Wyoming, is named for him (7, 4)
3. Product of Betsy Ross's needlework (8, 4)
6. Music genre of Ella Fitzgerald and Jelly Roll Morton (4)
8. "The Raven" author (5, 5, 3)
9. Early New York music publishing district (3, 3, 5)

Down

1. Thanksgiving dessert (7, 3)
2. Western fence with sharp points (6, 4)
4. Folk artist who took up painting in her 70s (7, 5)
5. "King of the Wild Frontier," in song (4, 8)
7. All-American sport played on a diamond (8)

Answer on page 253.

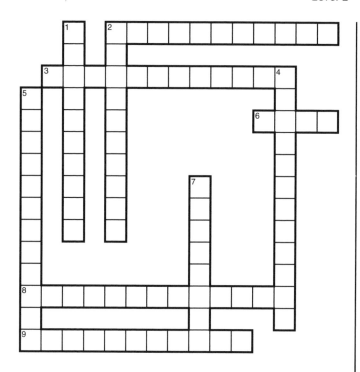

Name Calling

Decipher the encoded words in the "odd" definition below using the numbers and letters on the phone pad. Each number can stand for 3 or 4 possible letters.

Pathological: Being able

to 3–4–4–8–7–3 out how

to get out of a maze.

1	2 ABC	3 DEF
4 GHI	5 JKL	6 MNO
7 PQRS	8 TUV	9 WXYZ
	0	

LANGUAGE

CREATIVE THINKING

Between the Lines

Solve for the middle (undefined) word in each 3-word set. For each set, all 3 words appear on the same page in the dictionary in the order they are given. Rearrange the middle words to complete a quote from Sallust.

Example: putter: to work at random; tinker
puzzle
pygmy: one of a race of dwarfs

_ _ m m _ _ _: extinct Pleistocene mammal

_ _ _
_ _ _ _ g _: to handle or direct with a degree of skill

_ _ _ _ _ _ _ lago: a group of islands

_ _ _ _ _ _ _ _ _
_ _ _ _ _ v _: a repository or collection of information

_ _ r _ h: onward in time, place, or order
_ _ _ _ u _ _
_ _ _ _ _: the number equivalent to the product of 4
and 10

e _ _ _: always
_ _ _ _ y
_ _ _ _ _: to force out

_ w _ : chiefly nocturnal bird of prey with a large head
and eyes

_ _ _
_ x: a domestic bovine mammal

"_____ _____ is the _____ of his _____ _____."

Answers on page 253.

Masyu

Masyu has a simple goal: to draw a single, nonintersecting loop through all of the pearls on the grid.

There are 2 rules according to the color of the pearl.

Black pearls: A line must enter and exit at right angles from the pearl. It must also extend straight for 2 squares in the chosen direction.

White pearls: A line goes straight through each pearl and must turn immediately before or after. It is optional for the line to turn both before and after.

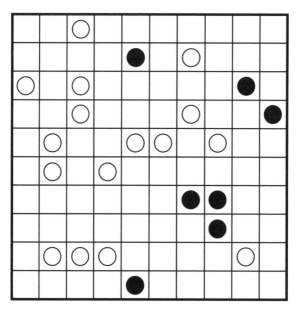

Hamster Treadmill

Only one of these exercise devices allows the hamster to run freely without the belts getting stuck. Is it device A or B?

A.

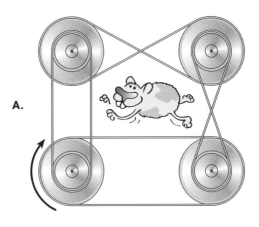

B.

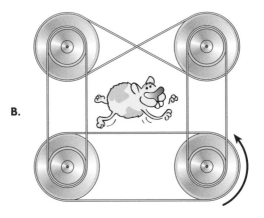

Answer on page 254.

Cross-Math

Place the digits 1 through 9 in the empty white squares so that the 3 horizontal and 3 vertical equations are true. Each digit will be used exactly once. Calculations are done from left to right and from top to bottom.

	+		+		=	15
+		×		÷		
	+		×		=	24
-		-		÷		
	+		-		=	14
=		=		=		
3		12		4		

Picasso Pizza (Part I)

Study this figure for 10 seconds, wait 1 minute, and then turn the page for a memory challenge.

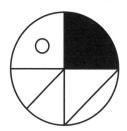

Answers on page 254. **61**

MEMORY

Picasso Pizza (Part II)

(Don't read this page before reading page 61!)

Which is the figure from the previous page?

A.   B.   C.   D.   E.

VISUAL SEARCH

Bird-Watching

Each horizontal row and vertical column contains the name of a bird. Find 18 birds by circling the correct letters in each row and column. All 81 letters in the grid are used—but only once.

LANGUAGE

J	H	E	O	A	G	D	L	E
E	O	D	M	P	T	U	H	L
R	R	O	W	H	O	U	A	K
S	N	W	A	E	I	C	N	A
F	L	A	M	A	I	N	G	O
H	B	O	E	S	N	K	W	R
A	I	C	L	A	R	O	K	W
G	L	V	U	N	T	L	L	K
Y	L	E	H	T	E	R	O	N

Answers on page 254.

1-2-3

Place the numbers 1, 2, and 3 in the circles below.
The challenge is to have only these 3 numbers in each
connected row and column—no number should repeat.
Any combination is allowed.

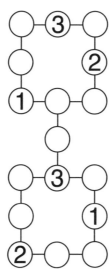

Tidy Up the Anagrams

What 2 words, formed from different arrangements of
the same 7 letters, can complete this sentence?

The _____ comedian used a whiskbroom to sweep the

"bunnies" under his bed into a _____.

VISUAL SEARCH

ATTENTION

SPATIAL VISUALIZATION

LANGUAGE

Find the Word

Ignoring spaces, capitalization, and punctuation, find all 14 occurrences of the consecutive letters S-O-F-A in this paragraph.

Russo, father of 2 and a calypso fan, went to see the boss of a small coffee shop for a job. The boss, a friendly fellow, had Russo fix an espresso fast without making a mess of anything. Russo twisted his torso far away from the hot flame and cooked a miso-flavored espresso faster than anyone the boss had ever seen. The boss, an alleged Mafioso fabled for his temper, loved the miso espresso far more than he expected. Insofar as Russo's chance of a job, the boss of another coffee shop also favored miso, and his offer was far more. Russo fared well and danced a calypso fancifully for his favorite customers.

A Puzzling Perspective

Mentally arrange the lettered balls from large to small in the correct order to spell an 11-letter word.

Clue: Awesomely

Answers on page 254.

Odd-Even Logidoku

The numbers 1 through 9 are to appear once in every row, column, long diagonal, irregular shape, and 3 by 3 grid. Cells marked with the letter **E** contain even numbers. Using the numbers given, complete the grid.

	6		E		E			2
E				E		E	7	
E	5	E		E				E
	E				E	E	E	
			E		E		E	E
E	E	E	E					
			E	E	E	E		
E		4	E		9		E	
1		E	E		3		8	E

Trivia on the Brain

The brain itself does not feel pain, so neurosurgeons can perform brain operations while patients are awake. An alert patient can then give the surgeon feedback to ensure a successful procedure.

Fists Are Flying

Across

1. NYC airport
4. "Phooey!"
8. Unit of mass
12. Foreman fighter
13. Got down
14. Acting part
15. TV Western set in Dodge City
17. Somewhat
18. Purchase made sight unseen
20. Abominable snowmen
23. Middle boy on "The Brady Bunch"
24. Mademoiselle's female friend
25. Pop pianist-singer Domino
28. Withdrew financial support
34. Military branch
35. New York college
36. Military or political staffers
40. Front steps
41. Sweet drink
45. Tear forcefully
46. Electrifying
50. _____ in a lifetime
51. "Finally, the weekend!"
52. Gidget portrayer Sandra
53. Nostradamus, some say
54. Feudal-class member
55. Night predator

Down

1. Drinking spree
2. Easily spread ailment
3. Family members
4. "Ghostbusters" actor Harold
5. Easy as falling off _____
6. Kind of torch
7. British gun
8. Wine fruit
9. Metal man
10. Identical
11. Taxi timer
16. Sales pitch
19. Basilica section
20. Mouth, in slang
21. Second-largest bird
22. "Shop _____ you drop"

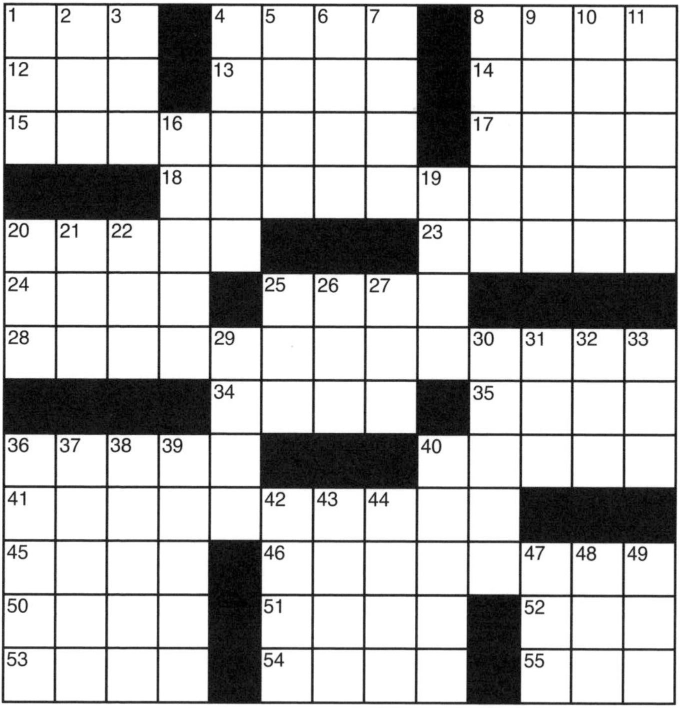

25. New Deal initiator
26. Holder of many $20 bills
27. Commandment pronoun
29. 90 degrees from north
30. Essential parts
31. Water closet
32. Colorful card game
33. Bridged distance
36. Hairstyles worn by Jimi Hendrix
37. "Me, Myself and _____" (Jim Carrey movie)
38. Conical-cap wearer
39. Duck with down
40. Scratch, as a baseball
42. Congratulates, in a way
43. Strong desire
44. Film _____
47. Wedding words
48. Hot off the press
49. Hair goo

SPATIAL REASONING

PLANNING

You Are Here

…and the taxi meter is ticking. This professional building is a maze of corridors and cubicles. Elevators are available, but there are no stairs. And over-stressed office workers won't give you directions to the exit. Why, oh why, did you ever come in here? Doesn't matter now—time to get moving!

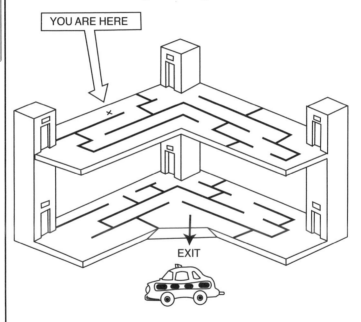

YOU ARE HERE

EXIT

Answer on page 255.

Hashi

Each circle represents an island, with the number inside indicating the number of bridges connected to it. Draw bridges between islands using the number given, but there can be no more than 2 bridges going in the same direction, and there must be a continuous

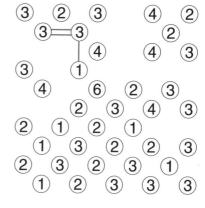

path connecting all islands. Bridges can be only vertical or horizontal and may not cross islands or other bridges. We've drawn some bridges to get you started.

Word Ladder

Use the clues to change just one letter on each line to go from the top word to the bottom word. Do not change the order of the letters. You must have a common English word at each step.

STOOL

_____ winds thread

_____ animal's leaving

_____ cutlery

_____ to faint

SWOOP

VISUAL LOGIC

SPATIAL VISUALIZATION

CREATIVE THINKING

CREATIVE THINKING

ANALYSIS

Puzzle Pieces

Visually fit these puzzle pieces together to form a square.

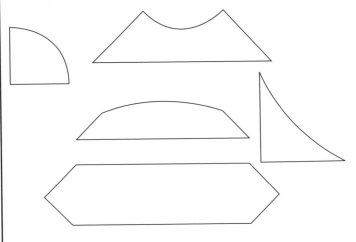

Short Sequence

Can you determine the missing letter?

MVEM __ SUN

Answers on page 255.

Vex-a-Gon

Place the numbers 1 through 6 into the triangles of each hexagon. The numbers may be in any order, but they do not repeat within each hexagon shape.

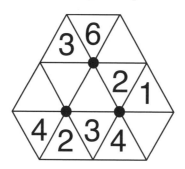

Name Calling

Decipher the encoded word in the quip below using the numbers and letters on the phone pad. Each number can stand for 3 or 4 possible letters.

What food these

6–6–7–7–3–5–7 be!

1	2 ABC	3 DEF
4 GHI	5 JKL	6 MNO
7 PQRS	8 TUV	9 WXYZ
	0	

Caroline's Word Search

Some people collect stamps, others coins. Our friend CAROLINE LOVELACE collects words with alternating consonants and vowels. Could this hobby have anything to do with her name? Or where she was born—the little Wisconsin town of OCONOMOWOC? Or the bumper sticker on her car, "LOVE ME LOVE MY DOG"? Join Caroline in searching for the 24 words and phrases below that have alternating consonants and vowels. The words can be found in a straight line horizontally or vertically. They may read either backward or forward. Leftover letters spell 4 additional words.

AMERICANA	MADAME BOVARY
APOLOGIZE	MEDICINE
CALAMITY JANE	NAVIGATOR
CAMERAMAN	PALOMINO
CAMISOLE	PARADOX
CARETAKER	PINAFORE
EMILE ZOLA	PINECONE
EXECUTIVE	POLICEMAN
FIGURINE	POLITICAL
JERUSALEM	RUTABAGA
LAZYBONES	SEMICOLON
LICORICE	VERONICA LAKE

```
B E A R O E N I R U G I F M E
T N E R Y N A M E C I L O P B
X O D A R A P O L I T I C A L
E C A S A J O R U T A B A G A
N E N E V Y L O P V P E L E R
O N A N O T O T A R I X O A G
L I C O B I G A L E N E Z E J
O P I B E M I G O K A C E L E
C E R Y M A Z I M A F U L O R
I S E Z A L E V I T O T I S U
M E M A D A L A N E R I M I S
E K A L A C I N O R E V E M A
S A C A M E R A M A N E B A L
O R A T E P A L I C O R I C E
R A L E G A L E N I C I D E M
```

Leftover letters spell: _____

_____

Homonyms

The clues "plunder" and "musical instrument" lead to which 2 words that sound alike but are spelled differently?

CREATIVE THINKING   LOGIC

Word Jigsaw

Fit the pieces into the frame to form common, uncapitalized words that read across and down. There's no need to rotate the pieces; they'll fit as shown, with each piece used exactly once.

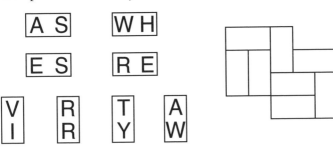

Sudoku

Use deductive logic to complete the grid so that each row, each column, and each 3 by 3 box contains the numbers 1 through 9 in some order. The solution is unique.

8		4		6		5		
	6			7			1	
7					1			9
			8				3	
3			6	2	4			5
	8				3			
5			1					2
	4			3			5	
		1		4		7		3

Answers on page 256.

Legion of **L**'s

We count 12 things in this picture that begin with the letter **L**. How many can you find?

VISUAL LOGIC

SPATIAL VISUALIZATION

CREATIVE THINKING

LANGUAGE

ANALYSIS

Mondrian-esque

The image below was inspired by the work of Dutch artist Piet Mondrian. How many squares of any size can you find in the figure?

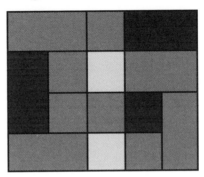

Wacky Wordy

Can you "read" the word below?

ANIC/EDAY

Answers on page 256.

Blind Ambition

Cryptograms are messages in substitution code. Break the code to reveal the quote and its source. For example, THE SMART CAT might become FVO QWGDF JGF if **F** is substituted for **T, V** for **H, O** for **E,** and so on.

" X I C S I E K S I J B F W B U D F

K U Z F D U W E, D P B J U S X L F I C X A F

X K G U P C W G I H F D F F J Z U L F

K V F M X N X M. "   — C X C E B U Z C X J

Odd One Out

Which of the words below doesn't belong?

Hint: Think about meanings.

BAT   MOLE
COW   KIWI

LANGUAGE

GENERAL KNOWLEDGE

Quic-Kross

This is a crossword puzzle with a twist. Use the clues to solve the puzzle. When complete, the circled letters will spell out a "mystery word."

Across
1. Mail
2. Edging
3. Animal flesh
4. Cute

Down
5. Agricultural enterprise
6. Country
7. Sodium chloride
8. Spherical object

Mystery word hint: Humiliating failure

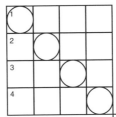

LOGIC

COMPUTATION

Calcu-doku

Use arithmetic and logic to complete the grid so that each row and column contains the numbers 1 through 5 in some order. Numbers in each outlined set of squares combine to produce the number in the top corner using the mathematical sign indicated.

4+		4×	10+	
5	4×		12×	
6+				20×
	2-		1	
1-		5	2/	

Answers on page 257.

Music Letterbox

The letters in the word UKULELE can be found in boxes 12, 16, 19, and 22, but not necessarily in that order. Similarly, the letters in the other musical instruments listed can be found in the boxes indicated. Your task is to insert all the letters into the grid. If you do this correctly, the names of 2 more instruments will be revealed in the shaded squares.

Hint: Compare BANJO and BASSOON to get the values of **J** and **S.** Then compare BASSOON and DOUBLE BASS to get the value of **N.**

BANJO: 5, 6, 7, 8, 21
BASSOON: 5, 6, 7, 20, 21
DOUBLE BASS: 5, 7, 14, 16, 19, 20, 21, 22
FLUTE: 10, 13, 16, 19, 22
OCARINA: 4, 5, 6, 7, 15, 23
ORGAN: 1, 5, 6, 7, 15
PICCOLO: 3, 4, 7, 19, 23
SAXOPHONE: 2, 3, 5, 6, 7, 11, 20, 22
TIN WHISTLE: 2, 4, 6, 9, 10, 19, 20, 22
TRUMPET: 3, 10, 15, 16, 17, 22
UKULELE: 12, 16, 19, 22
VIOLA: 4, 5, 7, 19, 24
XYLOPHONE: 2, 3, 6, 7, 11, 19, 22, 25
ZITHER: 2, 4, 10, 15, 18, 22

1	2	3	4	5	6	7	8	9	10	11	12	13
14	15	16	17	18	19	20	21	22	23	24	25	26
												Q

Triple-Jointed

Arrange these words and phrases in the grid on the next page. They fit only one way.

7 LETTERS
WELL-LIT

9 LETTERS
CHESS SETS
CLIFF FACE
FREE E-MAIL
STILL LIFE

10 LETTERS
DRESS SHIRT
FULL-LENGTH
GRASS SKIRT
SCOTT TUROW
SQUALL LINE
STIFF FINES
SWISS STEAK
YOU'LL LAUGH

11 LETTERS
CROSS SWORDS
MISS SCARLET
SEE EYE TO EYE

12 LETTERS
BRASS SECTION
BUSINESS SUIT
GLASS SLIPPER
SUCCESS STORY
WITNESS STAND

15 LETTERS
FOR GOODNESS SAKE
IN ALL LIKELIHOOD
IT'S A ZOO OUT
    THERE

16 LETTERS
SEAMLESS STOCKING

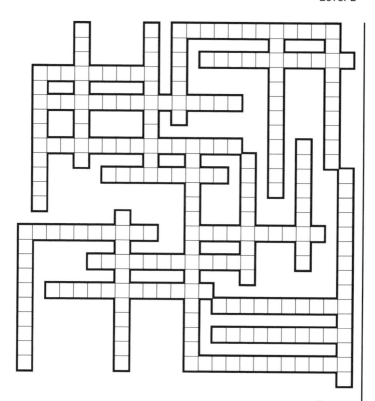

🔆 Trivia on the Brain

The average adult human brain weighs about 3 pounds and makes up about 2 percent of the total body weight. The heaviest brain ever recorded weighed 5 pounds, 1.1 ounces.

PROBLEM SOLVING ANALYSIS

Logic-cadabra!

Marvella, the world's greatest magician, challenged 2 women, Ann and Beth, to a test. Inside a pitch-black room were 5 headbands: 3 green and 2 yellow. The 3 women entered the room and each put on a headband. When they came out, they attempted to guess the color of their own headband (which they could not see), based on what the other women were wearing. To make it harder, Marvella wore her headband over her eyes so she could not see what colors the others were wearing. After they left the room, Ann looked at Beth and Marvella and said, "I don't know what color my headband is." Hearing this, Beth looked at Ann and Marvella and said, "I don't know what color my headband is, either." Marvella, with her own still covering her eyes, said, "I know what color mine is." What color is Marvella's headband?

LOGIC CREATIVE THINKING

Try Saying This Three Times Really Fast

Which day of the week is 2 days before the day after the day 3 days after the day before Tuesday?

Answers on pages 257–258.

Remember Me? (Part I)

Look at the objects below for 2 minutes, then turn the page and see how many of them you can remember.

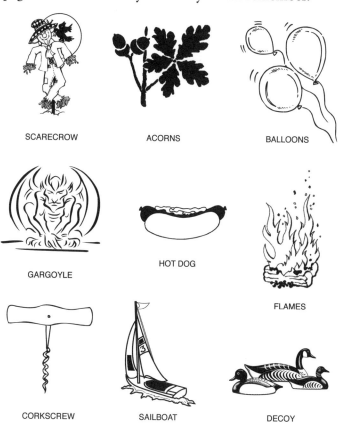

SCARECROW

ACORNS

BALLOONS

GARGOYLE

HOT DOG

FLAMES

CORKSCREW

SAILBOAT

DECOY

MEMORY

Remember Me? (Part II)

(Don't read this page before reading page 83!)

How many of the items listed below were pictured on the previous page?

Slipper	Tent	Acorns
Paintbrush	Hot Dog	Headset
Flames	Balloons	Scarecrow
Gargoyle	Goat	Decoy
Hula Hoop		

VISUAL LOGIC

Hitori

The object of this puzzle is to have numbers appear only once in each row and column. By shading a number cell, you are effectively removing that number from its row and column. There's a catch, though: Shaded number cells are never adjacent to one another in a row or column.

PLANNING

6	4	4	4	7	6	2	1
5	8	7	6	4	1	2	2
6	4	2	2	5	8	7	3
3	1	3	8	8	4	5	7
7	7	1	2	3	5	6	8
8	2	6	4	1	3	2	5
8	7	5	8	6	2	1	1
8	3	2	1	2	7	8	4

Answers on page 258.

Let It Shine by Alpha Sleuth™

Move each of the letters below into the grid to form common words. You will use each letter only once. The letters in the numbered cells of the grid correspond to the letters in the numbered squares below the grid, which constitute a phrase. Completing the grid will help you complete the phrase, and vice versa. When finished, you will have used all the letters in the letter set. The letters included in the grid will help you get started.

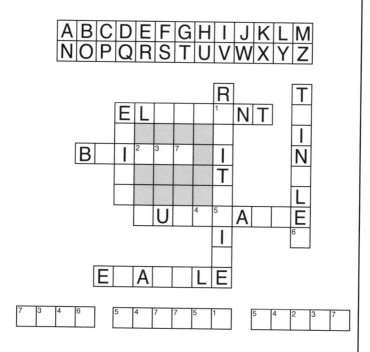

| A | B | C | D | E | F | G | H | I | J | K | L | M |
| N | O | P | Q | R | S | T | U | V | W | X | Y | Z |

VISUAL LOGIC

ANALYSIS

Revolutionary Event

A rebus follows its own type of alphabet: a mixture of letters, symbols, and pictures. Look carefully at the rebus below. You should be able to "read" the solution based on a clue in the title of the puzzle.

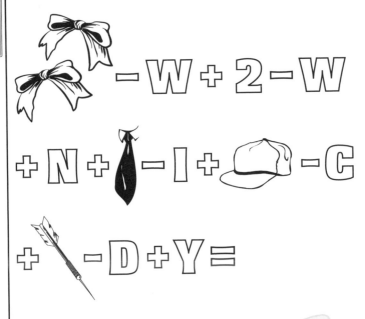

Trivia on the Brain

Approximately 20 percent of the oxygenated blood flowing from the heart is pumped to the brain.

Answer on page 258.

Sudoku

Use deductive logic to complete the grid so that each row, each column, and each 3 by 3 box contains the numbers 1 through 9 in some order. The solution is unique.

6	4			3	8	9		
			2	9			6	
		5	1					
5	6			4	3	8		2
9		8	6	5			3	4
				9	3			
	7			6	2			
		6	7	1			4	9

Sucker Bet

A local hustler at a bar in Atlantic City decided to take some money from the tourist sitting next to him. "See that couple over there?" he asked the guy. "They're married to each other, and their names are Vern and Shirley. I'll bet you $10 that Shirley has taken 2 trips to Atlantic City with her husband Vern, but Vern has only taken 1 trip to Atlantic City with his wife Shirley." The man thought this was impossible and took the bet. How did the hustler walk out of the bar with the visitor's sawbuck?

VISUAL SEARCH

ATTENTION

On Your Head

All of these words are contained within the group of letters below. They can be found horizontally, vertically, or diagonally, read backward or forward.

BERET   FEZ   PILLBOX

BONNET   HELMET   SOMBRERO

CAP   HOMBURG   STETSON

CLOCHE   HOOD   STRAW

DERBY   KEPI   TOPPER

FEDORA   PANAMA   TURBAN

FELT

```
F W A R T S H E L M E T
E D R O N O S T E T S X
D O Y G M M T L E F P O
O O T B E B E A N Y A B
R H U A R R E Z W R N L
A R R I P E K R E D A L
G Y B N E R D A E F M I
L P A C L O C H E T A P
B O N N E T R E P P O T
```

Answers on page 258.

Cube Quandary

In order for these 18 boards to form a regular cube, an individual board must have a certain ratio of its height, length, and width. What is that ratio?

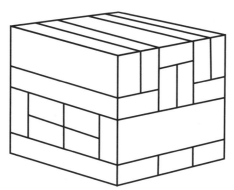

A President's Creed

Cryptograms are messages in substitution code. Break the code to read the quote and its source. For example, THE SMART CAT might become FVO QWGDF JGF if **F** is substituted for **T, V** for **H, O** for **E,** and so on.

" Q F G E   W   V N   A N N V ,   W   L G G J

A N N V .   Q F G E   W   V N   C H V ,   W   L G G J

C H V .   X F H X ' Y   T K   B G J W A W N E . "

—H C B H F H T   J W E D N J E

COMPUTATION

ANALYSIS

Number Crossword

Fill in this crossword with numbers instead of letters. Use the clues to determine which number from 1 through 9 belongs in each empty square. No zeros are used.

1	2		3	4
5		6		
	7			
8				9
10			11	

Across

1. A multiple of 11
3. A square number
5. Consecutive digits, descending
7. A square number
8. Consecutive odd digits, in some order
10. Digits add up to 4
11. A prime number

Down

1. A multiple of 12
2. A palindrome whose digits add up to 18
3. Consecutive odd digits, ascending
4. An even number
6. Consecutive digits, out of order
8. A multiple of 7
9. An odd number

Answers on page 259.

Rhyme Time

Each clue leads to a 2-word answer that rhymes, such as BIG PIG or STABLE TABLE. The numbers in parentheses after the clue give the number of letters in each word. As a bonus, can you figure out the theme for this puzzle?

1. Microsoft mogul Bill glides across the ice (5, 6):

   _____

2. Course of study taught by fashion designer Bill (5, 5):

   _____ _____

3. Cause "Groundhog Day" star Bill to fret (5, 6):

   _____ _____

4. "Shake, Rattle and Roll" singer Bill's Sunday through Saturday newspapers (6, 7): _____ _____

5. Former U.S. President Bill droppin' a clue (7, 6):

   _____ _____

Theme: _____

Trivia on the Brain

Scientists have actually identified the "oops" center of the human brain. We now know that there is a specific region of the brain that reacts when you realize you have made a mistake.

LOGIC

School Correction

Kenny is being punished for not completing his school assignments. His parents have listed his tasks for each of the next 4 days on the whiteboard, but Kenny has mixed them up. Each item is in the correct column, but only one entry in each column is correctly positioned. Here is what we know about the correct order:

1. Car is 1 place below cloth.
2. Brush is 1 place above clean.
3. Path is 2 places below wash.
4. Brush is not second.

Can you give the action, object, and tool for each position?

	Action	Object	Tool
1	paint	shed	roller
2	wash	car	cloth
3	sweep	path	brush
4	clean	floor	mop

☼ Trivia on the Brain

Although our bodies go to sleep, our brains do not. The brain remains as active all through the night as it is when you are awake.

Answers on page 259.

Who's Watching?

I set both my wife's watch and my watch at midnight. Later, I discovered that one of the watches went 2 minutes per hour too slow, and the other went 1 minute per hour too fast. When I looked at them later the same day, the faster one was exactly 1 hour ahead of the other.

What was the correct time when I looked at the watches?

Vex-a-Gon

Place the numbers 1 through 6 into the triangles of each hexagon. The numbers may be in any order, but they do not repeat within each hexagon shape.

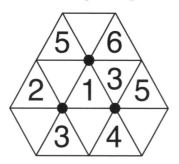

ANALYSIS · COMPUTATION · CREATIVE THINKING · PLANNING

Missing Connections

It's a crossword without the clues! Use the letters below to fill in the empty cells in the grid. When you are finished, you'll have words that read both across and down, crossword-style.

A A B D D E E E G L N O P R S T U X Y

Trivia on the Brain

The frontal lobes of your brain create feelings of self-awareness. Evidence suggests that children develop self-awareness at around 18 months of age.

Answers on page 259.

Arrow Web

Shade in some of the arrows in the grid so that each arrow points to exactly 1 shaded arrow.

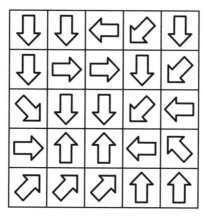

Upside Down and Backward

What 4-letter word, when printed in capital letters, reads the same upside down and backward?

Answers on page 259. 95

LANGUAGE

CREATIVE THINKING

Say What?

Below are a group of words that, when properly arranged in the blanks, reveal a quote from Issac Watts.

divine   demands   my   so   all   amazing   soul

"Love _____ _____, so _____, _____ my _____, _____

life, my _____."

CREATIVE THINKING

What a Racket

Can you determine the missing letter in this progression?

G, S, __

ANALYSIS

Answers on page 259.

Perfect Score

Make 3 successful hits so that the sum of the numbers is 100. Double and triple scores do not apply. Numbers may be used more than once.

Word Ladder

Use the clues to change just one letter on each line to go from the top word to the bottom word. Do not change the order of the letters. You must have a common English word at each step.

TRUCK

_____ or treat

_____ a pain in the neck

_____ sound of typed keys

_____ oily smoothness

_____ being lazy on the job

SNACK

Elevator Words

Like an elevator, words move up and down the "floors" of this puzzle. Starting with the first answer, the second word of each answer carries down to become the first word of the following answer. With the clues given, complete the puzzle.

1. Falls _____

2. _____ _____

3. _____ _____

4. _____ _____

5. _____ _____

6. _____ _____

7. _____ game

Clues

1. Virginia city near D.C.
2. Pew
3. Part of a weightlifter's routine
4. It will get a of member the media in for free
5. Super's door opener
6. Hotel guest's door opener
7. Bridge or rummy

Answers on page 260.

Twenty-four Jumble

Arrange the numbers and math signs in this cornucopia to come up with the number 24.

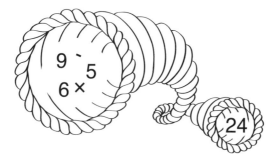

Liar's Logic

Use the following information to figure out who is lying and who is telling the truth. There are 2 truth-tellers and 2 liars. You know that A is a liar.

Person A says person C is lying.

Person B says person C is telling the truth.

Person C says person D is lying.

Person D says person A is telling the truth.

Answers on page 260.

Get It Straight

Don't get too caught up in all the twists and turns as you negotiate your way to the center of this intricate labyrinth.

Answer on page 260.

Sudoku

Use deductive logic to complete the grid so that each row, each column, and each 3 by 3 box contains the numbers 1 through 9 in some order. The solution is unique.

3	5		7		9	2	6	
			6	3	5			1
6		8				7	3	
2		4						
		5	4		8	6		
						9		3
	4	9				3		6
7			3	5	4			
	1	3	2		6		5	7

LOGIC

Anagram Snack

LANGUAGE

What 2 words, formed from different arrangements of the same 8 letters, can be used to complete the sentence below?

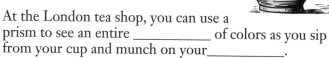

At the London tea shop, you can use a prism to see an entire _____ of colors as you sip from your cup and munch on your_____.

Rhyme Time

Each clue leads to a 2-word answer that rhymes, such as BIG PIG or STABLE TABLE. The numbers in parentheses after the clue give the number of letters in each word.

1. Single rifle or revolver (3, 3): _____

2. Opposable digit without sensation (4, 5):

   _____ _____

3. Cloistered man grew tiny (4, 6): _____ _____

4. Space telescope difficulty (6, 7): _____ _____

5. Shortness in duration of light humor (6, 7):

   _____ _____

Trivia on the Brain

It's no accident that many telephone numbers are 7 digits long. A person's short-term memory can process between 7 and 9 numbers at a time and store them just long enough to enable that person to at least find a phone.

Answers on page 260.

Cross-Math

Place the digits 1 through 9 in the empty white squares so that the 3 horizontal and 3 vertical equations are true. Each digit will be used exactly once. Calculations are done from left to right and from top to bottom.

	+		+		=	17
×		÷		+		
	÷		+		=	8
-		+		+		
	×		-		=	25
=		=		=		
10		7		18		

Word Jumble

Using letters from the 3 words below, create the shortest possible word in the English language.

Hint: The letter combinations MAR, AM, and FAR produce the word FARM.

ORIENTAL   OYSTER   SPORT

LOGIC

LANGUAGE

Crypto-botany

Cryptograms are messages in substitution code. Break the code to read the message. For example, THE SMART CAT might become FVO QWGDF JGF if **F** is substituted for **T, V** for **H, O** for **E,** and so on.

R H I E R H   (name of plant)

R C O J O   E J O   I H J O   U E J F O R F O N   H P

R H I E R H O N   R C E B   H P   E B W   H R C O J

U O M O R E L D O .   H J F M F B E D D W ,

O V J H K O E B N   R C H V M C R

R H I E R H O N   X O J O   K H F N H B H V N

E B G   M J O X   R C O I   E N   H J B E I O B R E D

K D E B R N .   R C O W   X O J O   M J H X B

L W   R C H I E N   A O P P O J N H B   F B

1 7 8 1 ,   L V R   X O J O B ' R   S B H X B   E N

E B   O G F L D O   P H H G   V B R F D   1 8 3 4 .

R H I E R H O N   C E U O   E D N H   L O O B

T E D D O G   M E J G O B   E K K D O ,   M H D G

E K K D O ,   E B G   D H U O   E K K D O .

Answer on pages 260–261.

Masyu

Masyu has a simple goal: to draw a single, nonintersecting loop through all of the pearls on the grid.

There are 2 rules according to the color of the pearl.

Black pearls: A line must enter and exit at right angles from the pearl. It must also extend straight for 2 squares in the chosen direction.

White pearls: A line goes straight through each pearl and must turn immediately before or after. It is optional for the line to turn both before and after.

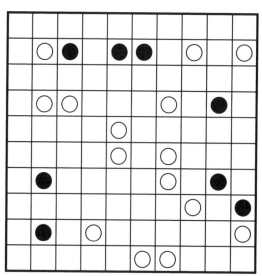

Fitting Words

PLANNING

GENERAL KNOWLEDGE

In this miniature crossword, the clues are listed randomly and are numbered for convenience only. It is up to you to figure out the placement of the 9 answers. To help you, we've inserted one letter in the grid, and this is the only occurrence of that letter in the puzzle.

Clues

1. World-weariness
2. Fascinated by
3. Luau dance
4. Play for time
5. The sum
6. Biting insect
7. Dusk to dawn
8. Cash drawer
9. Cardinal's home

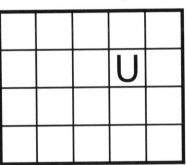

 Trivia on the Brain

Most people can remember between 5 and 9 digits at a time as long as they keep repeating the numbers to themselves. This is the limit of your working memory, which you use to remember things short-term.

Answers on page 261.

Get in Shape

Three of the 4 shapes below Figure 1 can be formed from cutting Figure 1 into 2 pieces and reassembling them. Which is the odd one out?

Fig. 1

A.

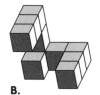

B.

C.

D.

CREATIVE THINKING

SPATIAL VISUALIZATION

VISUAL LOGIC

CREATIVE THINKING

LOGIC

Rich Riddle

Hoping to avoid spending a lot of money on little Johnny's birthday present, Grandpa offered to give him in dollars the largest 2-digit number he could think of. What's the most money Johnny could have received from Grandpa for his birthday?

PLANNING

LANGUAGE

Word Ladder

Use the clues to change just one letter on each line to go from the top word to the bottom word. Do not change the order of the letters. You must have a common English word at each step.

SMILE

_____ an old-fashioned, knightly physical blow

_____ mean-spiritedness, cruelty

_____ a tall tower that forms the roof of a building with a pointed top

_____ where the hobbits come from

_____ an item of clothing that often has a collar

_____ not tall

_____ things wash up on it

CHORE

LOGIC

ANALYSIS

Odd One Out

Which of the words below is the odd one out?

Hint: Think about sounds and meanings.

SITE   HERE
SENT   RIGHT

Answers on page 261.

ABCD

Place the letter A, B, C, or D in each square of the grid. The tables above and to the left of the grid indicate how many times each letter appears in that column or row. No letter can be horizontally or vertically adjacent to itself.

	A	B	C	D					
A	2	2	1	1	1	2			
B	2	0	2	2	2	1			
C	2	1	1	0	3	2			
A B C D	0	3	2	3	0	1			
2 1 1 2									
2 1 2 1									
1 2 2 1				A					
1 2 2 1									
2 1 2 1	A								
1 2 0 3									

1-2-3

Place the numbers 1, 2, and 3 in the circles below. The challenge is to have only these 3 numbers in each connected row and column—no number should repeat. Any combination is allowed.

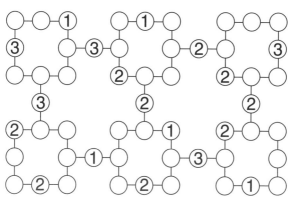

Answers on page 261. **109**

Acrostic

Solve the clues below and then place the letters in their corresponding spots in the grid to reveal a quote by a famous auto executive. The letter in the upper-right corner of each grid square refers to the clue the letter comes from. A black square indicates the end of a word.

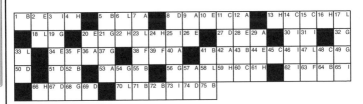

A. Author of quote (2 words)

___ ___ ___ ___ ___ ___ ___ ___ ___
42 57 29 36 12 53 9 40 7

B. Moves toward

___ ___ ___ ___ ___ ___ ___ ___ ___ ___
75 55 64 72 71 41 5 1 43 52

C. Most irritating pets?

___ ___ ___ ___ ___ ___
14 11 60 48 15 45

D. Huge

___ ___ ___ ___ ___ ___ ___
51 8 27 67 74 50 69

E. Hawing partner

___ ___ ___ ___ ___ ___ ___
20 28 34 44 2 10 26

Answers on page 261.

F. Horse's foot

— — — —
63 39 35 38

G. Scotland's third largest city

— — — — — — — —
54 56 37 68 32 21 49 19

H. Medieval musician

— — — — — — — —
66 24 16 13 59 61 4 22

I. Fly in the _____

— — — — — — — —
31 73 25 30 3 46 65 62

J. Scheming

— — — — — — — —
23 47 33 17 58 18 6 70

Hitori

The object of this puzzle is to have numbers appear only once in each row and column. By shading a number cell, you are effectively removing that number from its row and column. There's a catch, though: Shaded number cells are never adjacent to one another in a row or column.

8	3	1	7	2	6	8	5
1	1	1	8	3	7	2	4
6	7	7	7	4	3	3	8
7	5	3	2	1	7	4	6
1	4	5	3	6	2	7	5
4	7	6	5	2	8	3	2
8	6	4	7	8	1	2	3
3	2	2	1	5	4	6	3

PLANNING

VISUAL LOGIC

COMPUTATION | LOGIC

Break the Code

Determine the value of the symbols and find the missing number. It is the sum of the symbols, diagonally.

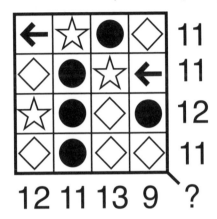

Cast-a-Word

PROBLEM SOLVING | LOGIC

There are 4 dice, and there are different letters of the alphabet on the 6 faces of each of them (each letter appears only once). Random throws of the dice produced the words in this list. Can you figure out which letters appear on each of the 4 dice?

BOLT	DOZE	OUCH	WANE
CAGE	JUNK	PALM	WARY
COAT	LOVE	RULE	SHIP
DANK	MAXI		

Answers on page 262.

Hamster Treadmill

Only one of these exercise devices allows the hamster to run freely without the belts getting stuck. Is it device A or B?

A.

B.

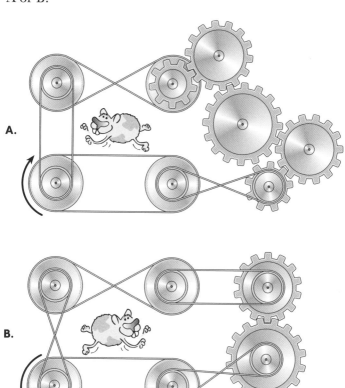

Answer on page 262. **113**

LANGUAGE / PLANNING

ANALYSIS / CREATIVE THINKING / COMPUTATION

Word Jigsaw

Fit the pieces into the frame to form common, uncapitalized words that read across and down crossword-style. There's no need to rotate the pieces; they'll fit as shown, with each piece used exactly once.

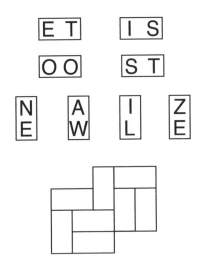

Think Twice

Can you complete the sequence?

166 86 46 26 16 __

Answers on page 262.

Cube Quandary

This diagram shows 6 connected squares that can be folded into a cube. Below the diagram are 4 views of the same cube. Can you fill in the 6 squares with the appropriate figures?

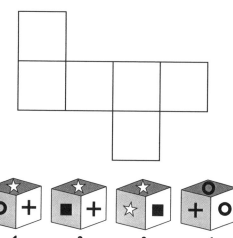

1   2   3   4

☼ Trivia on the Brain

You probably know that your brain is divided into two halves, or sides. But do you also know that the left side of your brain controls the right side of your body, and the right side of your brain controls the left side of your body?

Answer on page 262.

115

Hurry!

Across

1. Wild guess
5. Mont Blanc, e.g.
8. Did in
12. Columbus's home
13. Civil War general
14. Scruff
15. "Hurry!"
17. Like
18. One for the books?
19. Facet
21. Frittata
23. Circumspect
27. Small Pacific salmon
31. Aptly named fruit
32. Slow-witted
34. Presidential caucus state
35. Dark-meat choice
37. Bread crumbs, perhaps
39. Not slow-paced
41. Small bar
44. Kind of report

49. First place?
50. "Hurry!"
52. Matador's opponent
53. Sensitive subject,
    to some
54. Writer Ferber
55. Side order
56. Heir, perhaps
57. 49-Across inhabitant

Down

1. Counter order
2. Friends' pronoun
3. Isn't incorrect?
4. Two out of 2
5. Worried, and then some
6. Maui memento
7. Corolla part
8. "Hurry!"
9. Superior, e.g.
10. Like a DeMille
    production

11. Left
16. Club choice
20. Dry, as champagne
22. Ruler's decree
23. Kind of instinct
24. "That's disgusting"
25. Baba of "Arabian Nights"
26. "Hurry!"
28. ___ polloi
29. Fess (up)
30. Droop

33. Wet a little
36. Part of H.M.S.
38. Book written by Luke
40. Counter orders
41. Wagers
42. Superstar
43. Immunizing stuff
45. Word with code or rug
46. Mary Lincoln, nee ___
47. Arm bone
48. Bridge coup
51. Pride

ANALYSIS

Name Calling

Decipher the encoded word in the pun below using the numbers and letters on the phone pad. Each number can stand for 3 or 4 possible letters.

Kings worry about a

7–3–2–3–3–4–6–4 heir line.

1	2 ABC	3 DEF
4 GHI	5 JKL	6 MNO
7 PQRS	8 TUV	9 WXYZ
	0	

SPATIAL VISUALIZATION

A Puzzling Perspective

Mentally arrange the lettered balls from large to small in the correct order to spell an 11-letter word.

Clue: Defaulted debt

LANGUAGE

Answers on page 262.

Anagram Rhyme

The 2 phrases below are anagrams of phrases that are spelled differently and have different meanings but sound exactly alike (for example, "no notion" and "known ocean"). Find the 2 phrases.

fondle   shark   foul   dancers

Mixed Figures (Part I)

Study the figures below for one minute and then turn the page for a memory challenge.

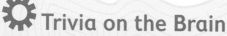

Trivia on the Brain

Have you heard that you only use 10 percent of your brain? That's not true! While you don't use all of your brain all of the time, the different parts you *do* use at different times add up to 100 percent.

Answer on page 262. **119**

MEMORY

Mixed Figures (Part II)
(Don't read this until you've read page 119!)

Which symbol on the previous page appeared twice?

SPATIAL REASONING

Exercise Time

PLANNING

You know you need to get out and walk more! Start at the dot on the left and take a little stroll.

Answers on pages 262–263.

Vex-a-Gon

Place the numbers 1 through 6 into the triangles of each hexagon. The numbers may be in any order, but they do not repeat within each hexagon shape.

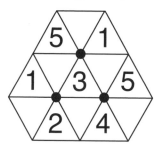

Odd-Even Logidoku

The numbers 1 through 9 are to appear once in every row, column, long diagonal, irregular shape, and 3 by 3 grid. Cells marked with the letter E contain even numbers. From the numbers given, can you complete the puzzle?

Star Power

Fill the empty squares in the grid so that each star is surrounded by the numbers 1 through 8 with no repeats.

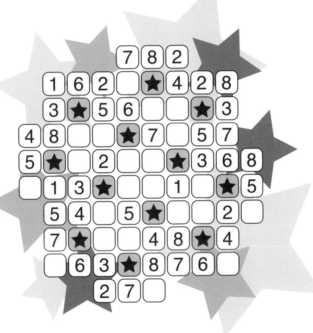

Answer on page 263.

Say What?

Below are a group of words that, when properly arranged in the blanks, reveal a quote from Leo Tolstoy.

own unhappy way families happy one family in

"All _____ _____ resemble _____ another, each

_____ _____ is unhappy _____ its _____ _____."

Liar's Logic

Use the following information to figure out who is lying and who is telling the truth. There are 3 truth-tellers and 2 liars.

Person A says person C is telling the truth.

Person B says person A is lying.

Person C says person B is lying.

Person D says person B is telling the truth.

Person E says person D is telling the truth.

Answers on page 263. 123

Cross Count

All the letters of the alphabet have been assigned a value from 1 through 9, as demonstrated in the box below. Fill in the grid with common words so that the rows and columns add up correctly.

1	2	3	4	5	6	7	8	9
A	B	C	D	E	F	G	H	I
J	K	L	M	N	O	P	Q	R
S	T	U	V	W	X	Y	Z	

²t				17
	¹a			17
a	³c	⁹		18
			⁴m	15
9	18	28	12	

Trivia on the Brain

A right-brain person tends to be more artistic, creative, and spontaneous. A left-brain person tends to be more logical, analytical, and controlled. Which side of your brain is more active for you?

LANGUAGE

COMPUTATION

Answers on page 263.

Kingdom of **K**'s

We count 11 things in this picture that begin with the letter **K**. How many can you find?

Ball Games

Across

1. Designate
4. Oil-burning light
8. It keeps the oxen together
12. Last word of the Pledge of Allegiance
13. One of the Muses
14. Winged Greek god
15. Ancestor of baseball
17. Air ball, e.g.
18. Marquette's title
19. "It's becoming clear"
21. Olympic sport since 1988
27. Diving bird
28. Heart medication
29. Lobbying group
32. Network connections
34. The wild blue yonder
35. Gasoline brand

37. Waffle topper
39. Game in which the target is called a "jack"
42. Lacking quality
43. Rainforest tree
46. Kind of camp
48. Canada's national summer sport
52. Leia's twin brother
53. Rubber stamp
54. "Don't open ___ Xmas"
55. Even scores
56. Passenger list entry
57. Sugary liquid

Down

1. Protective ground cover
2. Lotion additive
3. Speak suddenly
4. Type of TV screen
5. Alcoholic beverage
6. Former space station
7. Assume as a given
8. Mocha citizen
9. Points in the right direction
10. Puts on the canvas: abbr.
11. Double twist
16. Talk-radio host Boortz
20. Martial-arts instructor
22. Pygmy chimpanzee

23. London facility
24. Provide financial support for
25. Drive to distraction
26. Protein source
29. Crony
30. Physicians for Responsible Negotiations org.
31. Ranch hand
33. House alternation
36. $100 bills

38. Not taken in by
40. Acrylic
41. Tales of adventure
44. Where many Indians live
45. Form of seaweed
46. Club alternative, briefly
47. Nice affirmative
49. Sometimes called: abbr.
50. Motion transformer
51. Sandwich-bread choice

Hashi

Each circle represents an island, with the number inside indicating the number of bridges connected to it. Draw bridges between islands using the number given, but there can be no more than 2 bridges going in the same direction, and there must be a continuous path connecting all islands. Bridges can be only vertical or horizontal and may not cross islands or other bridges. We've drawn some bridges to get you started.

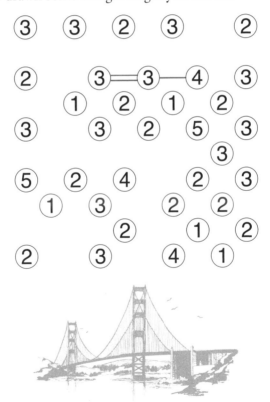

Answer on page 264.

Fitting Words

In this miniature crossword, the clues are listed randomly and are numbered for convenience only. It is up to you to figure out the placement of the 9 answers. To help you, we've inserted one letter in the grid, and this is the only occurrence of that letter in the completed puzzle.

Clues
1. Comedian's stock-in-trade
2. Suva's country
3. Recipe instruction
4. Element symbolized Fe
5. Really angry
6. Exam
7. Clumsy
8. Collect leaves
9. Original

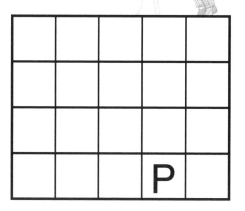

Between the Lines

Solve for the middle (undefined) word in each 3-word set. For each set, all 3 words appear on the same page in the dictionary in the order they are given. Rearrange the middle words to complete a quote from Germaine Greer.

Example: putter: to work at random; tinker
        puzzle
        pygmy: one of a race of dwarfs

i _ _ c t _ _ _: sedentary or passive
_ _ _ _ _ _ _ a b l e
_ _ _ _ _: lacking sense or significance; silly

_ _ g: to manipulate fraudulently
_ _ _ _ _
_ i _ _ _: stiff or unyielding

_ _ _: make a low, continuous, droning sound
_ _ _ _ a _
_ _ _ b _ _: not proud or arrogant; modest

_ h _ _ _: unifying or dominant idea
_ _ _ _ _ _ _ _ v e s
_ _ _ _: at that time

_ _ v _ _ _ _ _: an entrance designed to take
                    possession or overrun

_ _ _ _ _ _
_ _ _ _ r _ e: reversed in position, order, or direction

"_____ beings have an _____ _____ to _____ _____."

Answers on page 264.

Calcu-doku

Use arithmetic and
deductive logic to
complete the grid so
that each row and each
column contains the
numbers 1 through 5 in
some order. Numbers
in each outlined set
of squares combine to
produce the number
in the top corner using
the mathematical sign
indicated.

6×	7+	20×		5+
		1	3×	
7+		2		10×
6+	9+	15×		
			6×	

COMPUTATION LOGIC LANGUAGE PLANNING

Word Ladder

Use the clues to change just one letter on each line to go
from the top word to the bottom word. Do not change
the order of the letters. You must have a common
English word at each step.

JACKET

_____ a container

_____ a wooden strip that is part of a type of fence

_____ hit them to get a batsman out in cricket

_____ a woven fiber used to create furniture and
other objects

_____ evil

LICKED

LANGUAGE

Name that Scramblegram

Four 8-letter words, all of which revolve around the same theme, have been jumbled. Unscramble the 4 words and write the answers in the space next to each one. Then transfer the letters in the shaded boxes to the shaded row below and unscramble the 9-letter word that goes with the theme. The theme for this puzzle is women's names.

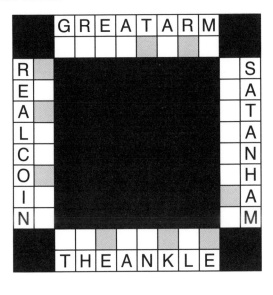

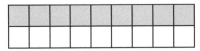

Answers on page 264.

World Cities Letterbox

The letters in LONDON can be found in boxes 3, 10, 16, and 26, but not necessarily in that order. The same is true for the other cities listed below. Insert all the letters of the alphabet into the boxes. If you do this correctly, the shaded cells will reveal another world city.

Hint: Look for words that share a single letter. For example, ROME shares only an **O** with SOFIA and only an **E** with QUEBEC. By comparing the number lists following these 3 words, you can deduce the values of the 2 shared letters.

BRUSSELS: 7, 9, 18, 19, 21, 26
COPENHAGEN: 1, 3, 4, 5, 6, 16, 18, 24
HELSINKI: 1, 8, 9, 13, 16, 18, 26
JAKARTA: 2, 6, 7, 13, 20
LONDON: 3, 10, 16, 26
MEXICO CITY: 3, 4, 8, 15, 18, 20, 22, 23
QUEBEC: 4, 14, 18, 19, 21
QUEZON CITY: 3, 4, 8, 14, 15, 16, 17, 18, 19, 20
REYKJAVIK: 2, 6, 7, 8, 11, 13, 15, 18
ROME: 3, 7, 18, 23
SANTIAGO: 3, 6, 8, 9, 16, 20, 24
SOFIA: 3, 6, 8, 9, 12
VILNIUS: 8, 9, 11, 16, 19, 26
WARSAW: 6, 7, 9, 25

1	2	3	4	5	6	7	8	9	10	11	12	13

14	15	16	17	18	19	20	21	22	23	24	25	26

Start Your Day by Alpha Sleuth™

PLANNING

LANGUAGE

Move each of the letters below into the grid to form common words. You will use each letter only once. The letters in the numbered cells of the grid correspond to the letters in the numbered squares below the grid, which constitute a phrase. Completing the grid will help you complete the phrase, and vice versa. When finished, you will have used all the letters in the letter set. The letters in the grid will help get you started.

Hint: The numbered cells in the grid are arranged alphabetically, so the letter in the cell marked 1 will appear in the alphabet before the letter in the cell marked 2, and so on.

A B C D E F G H I J K L M N O P Q R S T U V W X Y Z

134

Answers on page 265.

For Heavenly Navigators, a Star Maze

Navigate this maze in less than 1 minute and you will be a star, too.

PLANNING

SPATIAL REASONING

S

F

 Trivia on the Brain

Your ability to think and concentrate is affected by your senses, particularly your sense of smell. Jasmine can restore mental alertness, and rosemary can enhance mental performance. But any scents you associate with failure can make it difficult to concentrate and think clearly.

VISUAL LOGIC | COMPUTATION | PLANNING | LANGUAGE

Perfect Score

Make 3 successful hits so that the sum of the numbers is 100. Double and triple scores do not apply. Numbers may be used more than once.

Word Ladder

Use the clues to change just one letter on each line to go from the top word to the bottom word. Do not change the order of the letters. You must have a common English word at each step.

GLOSS

_____ window material

_____ a common plant

_____ crude

_____ social standing

CLASP

Answers on page 265.

Cross-Math

Place the digits 1 through 9 in the empty white squares so that the 3 horizontal and 3 vertical equations are true. Each digit will be used exactly once. Calculations are done from left to right and from top to bottom.

	+		-		=	11
+		÷		+		
	+		+		=	15
-		+		+		
	+		-		=	11
=		=		=		
1		9		11		

Whistling Workers

Can you determine the missing letter?

D G H S __ S D

Hangin' 10

This grid contains words used by surfers (listed on the next page). They can be found in a straight line horizontally, vertically, or diagonally and may be read either backward or forward. Leftover letters spell a quip.

```
D  U  D  E  Y  O  U  J  S  H  P  D  R  O  U
D  E  X  A  L  E  X  A  A  L  I  D  E  K  N
D  R  E  V  I  U  Q  O  W  K  P  T  V  C  H
U  A  A  T  A  A  C  S  S  W  E  L  L  T  K
C  D  K  I  R  I  P  C  U  R  L  G  I  C  K
K  I  D  I  P  A  I  V  K  C  I  T  S  S  A
D  C  A  E  N  S  L  F  A  D  N  U  K  N  U
I  A  D  R  K  E  F  U  G  L  E  O  I  E  F
V  L  O  B  R  O  D  E  B  O  S  E  U  T  A
E  R  H  R  G  H  T  U  T  U  D  P  Q  G  A
N  D  A  N  A  S  Q  S  D  C  T  I  E  N  U
I  B  I  L  L  A  B  O  N  G  H  W  V  A  E
M  O  O  R  N  E  E  R  G  R  I  S  A  H  K
G  M  C  O  Y  L  R  A  N  G  L  L  E  C  T
E  B  U  T  I  O  N  O  F  S  T  I  C  K  S
```

Leftover letters spell: _____

_____

AXELAXED

BARREL

BILLABONG

BOMB

DA KINE

DECK

DUCK DIVE

DUDE

EPIC

FETCH

GIDGET

GNARLY

GOING OFF

GREEN ROOM

HANG TEN

HODAD

JAKE

LEASH

PIPELINE

QUIKSILVER

QUIVER

RADICAL

RAIL

RIP CURL

STICK

STOKED

SWELL

TUBE

TUBULAR

VALSPEAK

WIPEOUT

Quic-Kross

This is a crossword puzzle with a twist. When complete, the circled letters will spell out a "mystery word."

Across

1. Bleed (past tense)
2. Say (past tense)
3. Decorative edging
4. Storage display

Down

5. Sleigh
6. Spherical adornment
7. A type of moss
8. Precise

Mystery word hint: Rear position

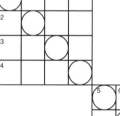

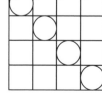

PLANNING

COMPUTATION

Number Maze

Find your way through the maze. Start with the 7 in the upper left corner and finish with the 8 in the lower right corner. Move only through spaces containing numbers that are multiples of either 7 or 8.

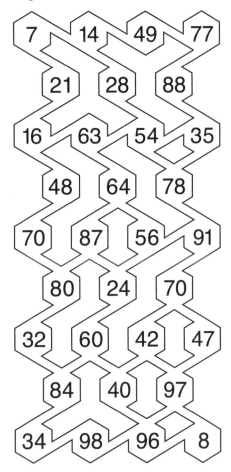

7 14 49 77

21 28 88

16 63 54 35

48 64 78

70 87 56 91

80 24 70

32 60 42 47

84 40 97

34 98 96 8

Answer on page 266.

Word Jigsaw

Fit the pieces into the frame to form common, uncapitalized words that read across and down. There is no need to rotate the pieces; they'll fit as shown, with each piece used exactly once.

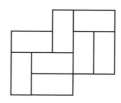

Digital Sudoku

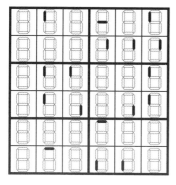

Fill in the grid so that each row, column, and 2 by 3 box contains the numbers 1 through 6 exactly once. Numbers are in digital form. Some segments have been filled in.

ANALYSIS | PROBLEM SOLVING

Trifling Truffles

Chuck, the CEO of a growing company, had to buy gifts for 5 employees on Administrative Professionals Day. Being a busy man with little time to shop, he went to a local candy store to pick up boxes of 8 cream-filled truffles for each of his 5 assistants. Chuck picked out 10 truffles of each flavor—cherry, fudge, vanilla, and maple—and asked the clerk to make sure the boxes contained 1 of each flavor and that each box had a different combination of candies (he wanted his assistants to think they'd received a special box).

Chuck handed out the boxes of truffles and went back to his office. His employees immediately opened their gifts to compare candies. Astra found that she had received an equal number of cherry- and fudge-filled truffles. Bunny had twice as many vanilla creams as fudge-filled. Coco's total number of maple and vanilla creams was the same as her total number of cherry and fudge. Danielle found she had fewer cherry creams than any other flavor. Evie's box of truffles had more maple creams than all other creams put together. How many cream-filled truffles of each flavor did each assistant receive?

Answer on page 266.

Hashi

Each circle represents an island, with the number inside indicating the number of bridges connected to it. Draw bridges between islands using the number given, but there can be no more than 2 bridges going in the same direction, and there must be a continuous path connecting all islands. Bridges can only be vertical or horizontal and may not cross islands or other bridges. We've drawn some bridges to get you started.

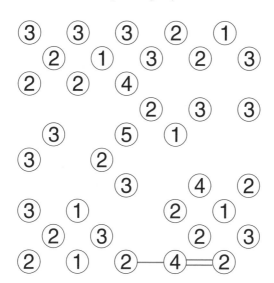

Star Power

Fill the empty squares in the grid so that each star is surrounded by the numbers 1 through 8 with no repeats.

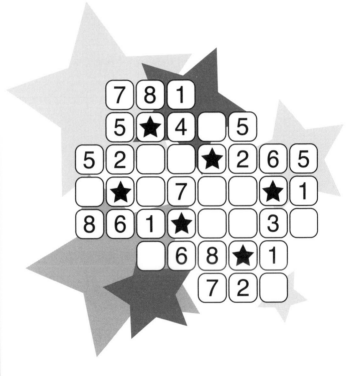

144

Answer on page 267.

ANALYSIS

The Whys and Wherefores

If X and Y are different positive digits, the value of Y could be from 2 to what number?

COMPUTATION

$$
\begin{array}{r}
Y4 \\
Y8 \\
+\ X6 \\
\hline
148
\end{array}
$$

Beautiful Words (Part I)

MEMORY

The words below been have been cited as among the most beautiful words in the English language. Study them for a few minutes and then turn the page to see how many you can recall.

ANEMONE   TRANQUIL

MURMURING   LUMINOUS

MELODY   MOTHER

ORIOLE   MELLIFLUOUS

LULLABY   GOSSAMER

Answer on page 267.

MEMORY

Beautiful Words (Part II)

(Don't read this until you've read page 145!)

Check off the words you recall from the preceding page.

___ GOLDEN   ___ OLEANDER

___ MELODY   ___ TRANQUIL

___ HALCYON   ___ MURMURING

___ DAMASK   ___ LAUGHTER

___ GOSSAMER   ___ ORIOLE

ANALYSIS

Name Calling

Decipher the encoded words in the quip below using the numbers and letters on the phone pad. Each number can stand for 3 or 4 possible letters.

"7–8–7–4" and "7–8–5–5" are 9–7–4–8–8–3–6 on the 3–6–6–7 of 7–8–2–2–3–7–7.

1	2 ABC	3 DEF
4 GHI	5 JKL	6 MNO
7 PQRS	8 TUV	9 WXYZ
	0	

Answers on page 267.

Cube Quandary

Which among cubes **A** through **E** is incorrect? What does the missing face of cube **F** look like?

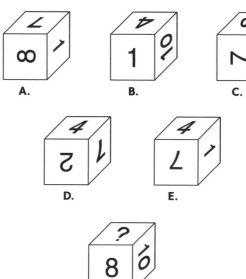

A.

B.

C.

D.

E.

F.

☼ Trivia on the Brain

The human brain is about 75 percent water. Your brain relies on micronutrients (antioxidants) from fruits and vegetables to safeguard its cells from damage and dysfunction.

VISUAL SEARCH
ATTENTION

Find the Word

Ignoring spaces, capitalization, and punctuation, find all 12 occurrences of the consecutive letters T-R-A-P in the paragraph below.

Nice T, rapper extraordinaire, rapped at rapid-fire speeds for his rapt fans. Apt rapper Master Apple toured with Nice T, rapping and filling in as an extra person in the band. At a concert, T accidentally ran into the orchestra pit, and Master Apple became a hit rapping in his place. Nice T repeated his mantra, "Please Let Me Rap" and returned as an ultra performer, topping the charts again and trampling Apple in his wake. Apple got rapiers and challenged T to a rapper duel, but T apologized, and Apple and T rapidly became friends and duet rappers again.

LANGUAGE
COMPUTATION

Cross Count

All the letters of the alphabet have been assigned a value from 1 through 9, as demonstrated in the box. Fill in the grid with common English words so that the rows and columns add up correctly. The completed grid will contain the name of a Greek letter.

1	2	3	4	5	6	7	8	9
A	B	C	D	E	F	G	H	I
J	K	L	M	N	O	P	Q	R
S	T	U	V	W	X	Y	Z	

7	5	1	13
			10
			20
24	15	4	

Answers on page 267.

Famous Address

Complete the horizontal phrase by finding the merging phrases.

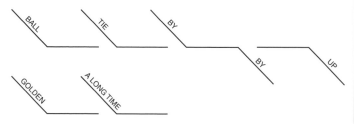

Read Between the Lines

Which figure among A through D comes next?

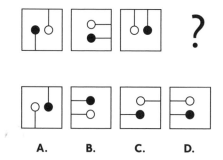

A.   B.   C.   D.

LEVEL 4 **Feel the Burn**

Mondrianize It!

Inspired by the work of Dutch artist Piet Mondrian, this puzzle consists of stars and circles. Using the checkered pattern as a guide, draw in lines so that each star is in its own square and each circle in its own rectangle.

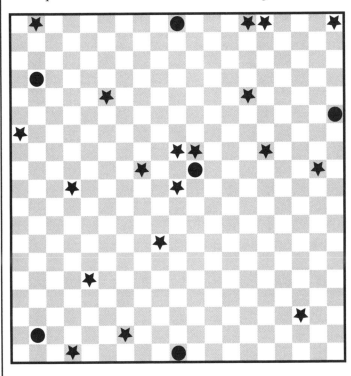

Answer on page 268.

Figure This Out

Which figure is different from the others?

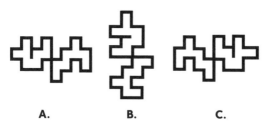

A. **B.** **C.**

D. **E.**

Memory Test with a Twist (Part I)

All of these words have something in common. Study and remember them. Take your time and try to determine the common feature. When you are ready, turn the page and see how many you can recall.

CRABCAKE   HIJACK

INDEFINITE   DOORSTOP

LAUGHING   ASTUTE

CALMNESS   MONOPOLY

SOMNOLENT   AFGHANISTAN

Answer on page 268. **151**

ANALYSIS

LOGIC

MEMORY

MEMORY

Memory Test with a Twist (Part II)

(Don't read this page until you've read page 151!)

What is common among the words on the previous page, and which of these do you recall from that page?

___ CALMNESS	___ MEANDERING
___ PAVEMENT	___ CRAB APPLE
___ PLUTOCRAT	___ INCREDIBLE
___ SOMNOLENT	___ AFGHANISTAN
___ LAUGHING	___ ASTUTE

LOGIC

COMPUTATION

Go Figure

Fill each square in the grid with a number from 1 through 6. When the numbers in each row are multiplied, you should arrive at the total in the right-hand column. When the numbers in each column are multiplied, you should arrive at the total on the bottom

						144
2	3	4	1	3		288
	2			1	2	72
6		2	3		4	1440
	3	6	2	5	1	360
4	1	2	3		3	432
	6	4	4	3	4	2304

576 540 384 432 540 384 384

line. The numbers in each long diagonal must multiply to the totals in the upper and lower right corners.

Answers on page 268.

Masyu

Masyu has a simple goal: to draw a single, nonintersecting loop through all of the pearls on the grid.

There are 2 rules according to the color of the pearl.

Black pearls: A line must enter and exit at right angles from the pearl. It must also extend straight for 2 squares in the chosen direction.

White pearls: A line goes straight through each pearl and must turn immediately before or after. It is optional for the line to turn both before and after.

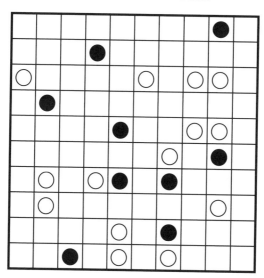

Help Find Our Missing Circus Acts!

These 9 two-word phrases are acts you might find at a circus. But we've made a few changes. First, we removed 1 letter from each word (it's the same letter for both words). Then we jumbled up the remaining letters. Your job is to figure out which letter is missing from each side and to put it on the center line. For example, CUSRI ___ WOLN, might reveal that a **C** is missing from both sides. When you add it to both words, they can unscramble to read CIRCUS CLOWN. When read from top to bottom, the missing letters will spell out a tenth circus act—one of the most exciting.

ITTS ___ KAWRE

RALEA ___ BTACSCROA

DRSW ___ WREALLSW

MAUH ___ LLBAOCNAN

ZEEPRA ___ STRIA

CIMG ___ CT

CIUS ___ RESROFERP

RABKCAB ___ DIRR

UNTEFO ___ LELET

Answers on page 268.

Oddball of the Group

Which figure is the odd one out?

1.   **2.**   **3.**

4.   **5.**

Word Ladder

Use the clues to change just one letter on each line to go from the top word to the bottom word. Do not change the order of the letters.

PUNCH

_____ a cluster

_____ sit on it in a park

_____ more of it with the tide out

_____ a sweet fruit

PEACE

CREATIVE THINKING

SPATIAL VISUALIZATION

VISUAL LOGIC

LANGUAGE

PLANNING

Answers on page 269.

That's a Hot One

Across

1. Mock
5. "_____ homo"
9. Agent 99's husband
12. Cruising, perhaps
13. Crowd noise
14. Penny portrait
15. Device using a magnetron
18. Early form of plastic
19. Gov't meat grader
20. Biblical site
21. Actress-turned-poker-player Tilly
23. Bushranger Kelly
25. Cleared course
29. Metal-lined fireplace
33. Overdue book fine
34. Uncooked
35. Don't dawdle
36. Netflix deliveries
39. Passing notice
42. Baked Alaska filling
46. Best in one's class
48. Deuce
49. Cry of mock horror
50. Bump into
51. Familiar
52. Stuns
53. Puts in

Down

1. Door section
2. Polo field?
3. Ate like a bird?
4. Dog or flop ending
5. Monroe's "The Seven Year Itch" co-star
6. Blazer
7. Alley Oop, e.g.
8. Before, in poetry
9. Dallas players, for short
10. Out for the night?
11. Lucy Lawless part
16. Spanish cheer
17. Word of obligation
22. Martians, e.g.

¹	²	³	⁴	■	⁵	⁶	⁷	⁸	■	⁹	¹⁰	¹¹

23. Organization covering 2 conferences
24. Baseball pitcher's stat
25. Dessert sometimes served a la mode
26. Went downhill
27. Actress Gardner
28. Ground hemlock
30. "Super duper!"
31. Col. Sanders's chain
32. "Don't dwell on the past"

36. Monopoly documents
37. Tape machine: abbr.
38. Excitement
39. Football great Graham
40. College football game name
41. Ubiquitous music player
43. Portion of tobacco
44. Like fine Scotch
45. Subway Series team
47. Word in a U.S. Marines slogan

Answers on page 269.

Number Crossword

Fill in this crossword with numbers instead of letters.
Use the clues to determine which of the numbers
1 through 7 belongs in each square. No zeros are used.

Across
1. A square number
3. 1-Across times 1-Down
6. Four different digits
7. A square number

Down
1. A multiple of 87
2. Three identical digits
4. A multiple of 17
5. A square number

Wacky Wordy

Can you "read" the word below?

TOM OOOOOOOO

Answers on page 269.

More Fun than a Barrel of Grapes

This maze is said to have been carved into a wine barrel by vineyard workers who wanted a break from picking grapes.

LANGUAGE

GENERAL KNOWLEDGE

Elevator Words

Like an elevator, words move up and down the "floors" of this puzzle. Starting with the first answer, the second word from each answer carries down to become the first word of the following answer. With the clues given, complete the puzzle.

Clues

1. Rocky road, e.g.   1. ice _____

2. Bagel topper   2. _____ _____

3. Curd shaper   3. _____ _____

4. Where the media sits   4. _____ _____

5. Disposable shooter?   5. _____ _____

6. Suitable for scanning   6. _____ _____

7. Off the rack   7. _____ made

☼ Trivia on the Brain

Feeling down and need a little pick-me-up? Chocolate contains phenylethylamine—the same chemical your brain releases when you're in love. No wonder eating sweets makes us feel good!

Answers on page 269.

Odd-Even Logidoku

The numbers 1 through 9 are to appear once in every row, column, long diagonal, irregular shape, and 3 by 3 box. Cells marked with the letter **E** contain even numbers. From the numbers given, can you complete the puzzle?

Vex-a-Gon

Place the numbers 1 through 6 into the triangles of each hexagon. The numbers may be in any order, but they do not repeat within each hexagon shape.

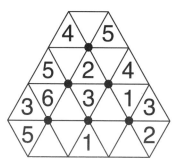

Hashi

Each circle represents an island, with the number inside indicating the number of bridges connected to it. Draw bridges between islands using the number given, but there can be no more than 2 bridges going in the same direction, and there must be a continuous path connecting all islands. Bridges can be only vertical or horizontal and may not cross islands or other bridges.

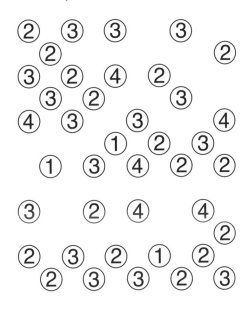

Answer on page 270.

Name Calling

Decipher the encoded words in the quip below using the numbers and letters on the phone pad. Each number can stand for 3 or 4 possible letters.

1	2 ABC	3 DEF
4 GHI	5 JKL	6 MNO
7 PQRS	8 TUV	9 WXYZ
	0	

A 4–8–3–7–8 is like the rain:

When he 7–3–7–7–4–7–8–7,

he is a 6–8–4–7–2–6–2–3.

A Puzzling Perspective

Mentally arrange the lettered balls from large to small in the correct order to spell an 11-letter word.

Clue: To spit

LANGUAGE | **PLANNING**

Word Columns

Find the dialogue from a classic TV show by using the letters directly below each blank square. Each letter is used only once. Black squares indicate the end of a word.

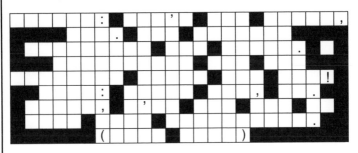

```
                              r
        o         a          y         y
      i s m     a h r u T   s o t     w
    u t t i     e t z n k s y o d   o o
  t a i t e r S S n e p s t a s n n y l o
  r o o h t e s a A l e e d y n u a t s e
  a a c r k m p T h o l e d a r I n I h r r A
S S K k e y t t t d a l n r e k u a m M u r s
t c c t n i a h I c l a l r r I e e d t y t o
```

Trivia on the Brain

After you are 30 years old, your brain shrinks a quarter of a percent in mass each year.

Answer on page 270.

1-2-3

Place the numbers 1, 2, and 3 in the circles below. The challenge is to have only these 3 numbers in each connected row or column—no number should repeat. Any combination is allowed.

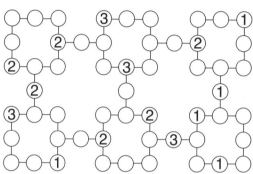

Fitting Words

In this miniature crossword, the clues are listed randomly and are numbered for convenience only. It is up to you to figure out the placement of the 9 answers. To help you, we've inserted one letter in the grid, and this is the only occurrence of that letter in the puzzle.

1. Bloke
2. Detest
3. Uses the keyboard
4. _____ and crafts
5. Inclined
6. Toe the line
7. Coffee + chocolate
8. Fine-tune
9. Rat's nosh, in the house that Jack built

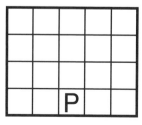

Find It

This is a word search with a twist. Instead of giving you a list of words to find, we've provided a list of categories. Your challenge is to find 3 items for each category within the group of letters on the next page. The words can be found horizontally, vertically, or diagonally. They may read either backward or forward.

3 SHADES OF BLUE

_____

_____

_____

3 THINGS THAT
ARE ROUND

_____

_____

_____

3 BASEBALL TERMS

_____

_____

_____

3 ONE-WORD MOVIES
STARTING WITH "T"

_____

_____

_____

3 U.S. CAPITAL CITIES

_____

_____

_____

```
X E U R G G D L O D
S I N M E N F A R O
T S A P P H I R E D
H T A B S I C R T E
C O G L N Y R T S N
A O D D E O O E I P
O T I N Q M T T W P
Y G A N I R S S T M
O V P Z C U E S O Y
Y R I D A Y H S C B
```

Sequencing

What 3-digit number comes next?

481, 216, 202, 428, 323, __

ANALYSIS CREATIVE THINKING

Orbiting Orbs

Fill in the blank spaces as you would in a crossword puzzle. The theme—or title—of the puzzle might appear to be ambiguous, but it should suggest a category of words that, when linked together, will complete the puzzle.

For example, HOLE IN ONE might suggest DOUGHNUTS. Or it might suggest GOLF, which would lead to the words CLUB, IRON, TEE, etc. But all of these words have a common theme. Notice that a few letters are already in place, and some of the words intersect—which just adds to the mystery, and the fun, of finding the solution.

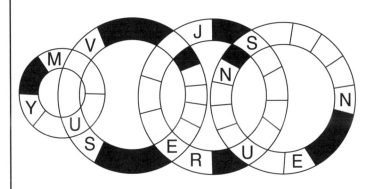

Answer on page 270.

Code-doku

Solve this puzzle just as you would a sudoku. Use deductive logic to complete the grid so that each row, column, and 3 by 3 box contains the letter combinations NO GLUM REV. When you have completed the puzzle, read the shaded squares to reveal a name and 2 words.

	N	U	O					
L		G						N
V					N	O		
				G				U
					R	E		
	G	O		M				
R			L	V			U	
		E			O	N		
	L							

It's a Song

Reveal the horizontal phrase by completing the merging phrases.

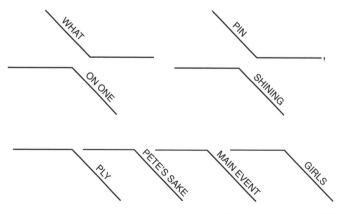

WHAT

ON ONE

PIN

SHINING

PLY   PETE'S SAKE   MAIN EVENT   GIRLS

Kakuro

Place a number from 1 through 9 in each empty cell so that the sum of each vertical or horizontal run (rows and columns extending from the numbered cells) equals the number at the top or to the left of that run. Numbers may not be repeated in any run, and runs end at dark-colored squares.

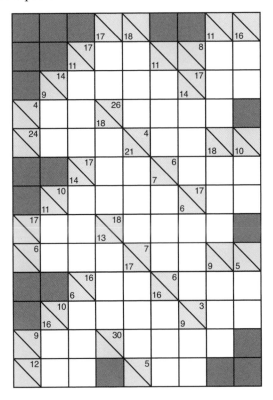

Answer on page 271.

Perfect Score

Make 3 successful hits so that the sum of the numbers is 100. Double and triple scores do not apply. Numbers may be used more than once.

Word Ladder

Use the clues to change just one letter on each line to go from the top word to the bottom word. Do not change the order of the letters. You must have a common English word at each step.

HILL

_____ the handle of a sword

_____ stop

_____ a mark of purity

_____ large room for assembly

_____ one of the bladders

_____ a forceful wind

PALE

LOGIC

Digital Sudoku

Fill in the grid so that each row, column, and 2 by 3 box contains the numbers 1 through 6 exactly once. Numbers are in digital form, and some segments have been filled in.

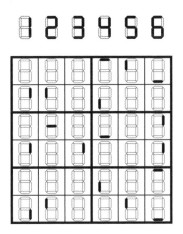

🔆 Trivia on the Brain

Have you ever searched for something for an hour, only to find it was sitting in front of you the whole time? Your brain doesn't always see everything your eyes take in. Magicians rely on this trick when performing some of their illusions.

Answer on page 271.

Rhyme Time

Each clue leads to a 2-word answer that rhymes, such as BIG PIG or STABLE TABLE. The numbers in parentheses after the clue give the number of letters in each word.

1. Old-fashion watch (4, 4): _____

2. A dive over the line for a touchdown (4, 4): _____

3. Overheated college residence (4, 4): _____

4. Swindle on the tracks (4, 4): _____

5. Swine utensil (4, 4): _____

6. Antique-store purchase (4, 5): _____

7. A most impressive bird of prey (5, 5): _____

8. Sugar cookie (5, 5): _____

9. Clique within the cast (6, 5): _____

10. In-crowd's favorite flick (6, 5): _____

11. Temporary crown (6, 6): _____

12. Roach-race timer (7, 5): _____

The Upper Crust
by Alpha Sleuth™

Move each of the letters below into the grid to form common words. You will use each letter only once. The letters in the numbered cells of the grid correspond to the letters in the numbered squares below the grid, which constitute a phrase. Completing the grid will help you complete the phrase, and vice versa. When finished, you will have used all the letters in the letter set. The letters in the grid will help get you started.

Hint: The numbered cells in the grid are arranged alphabetically, so the letter in the cell marked 1 will appear in the alphabet before the letter in the cell marked 2, and so on.

A B C D E F G H I J K L M N O P Q R S T U V W X Y Z

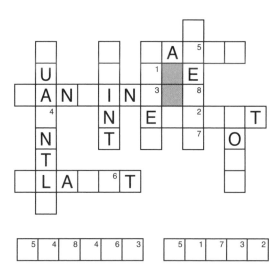

Answers on page 271.

Vex-a-Gon

Place the numbers 1 through 6 into the triangles of each hexagon. The numbers may be in any order, but they do not repeat within each hexagon shape.

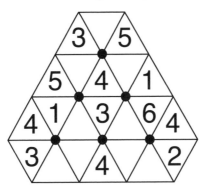

Cast-a-Word

There are 4 dice, and there are different letters of the alphabet on the 6 faces of each of them (each letter appears only once). Random throws of the dice produced the words in this list. Can you figure out which letters appear on each of the 4 dice?

AXED	GOWN	RICE
BLED	MALE	RUST
DECK	OVER	VINE
DUKE	PELT	WHIP
FAIL	PLOY	ZEAL

Answers on pages 271–272.

CREATIVE THINKING | PLANNING

LOGIC | PROBLEM SOLVING

VISUAL LOGIC

PLANNING

Hitori

The object of this puzzle is to have numbers appear only once in each row and column. By shading a number cell, you are effectively removing that number from its row and column. There's a catch, though: Shaded number cells are never adjacent to one another in a row or column.

2	2	2	4	5	7	3	3
2	7	6	6	1	8	2	3
1	5	8	2	4	3	7	4
5	1	3	4	4	6	2	8
6	3	2	7	4	4	5	7
8	4	6	1	3	8	6	5
4	2	5	6	3	1	1	7
3	6	5	8	7	5	4	1

☼ Trivia on the Brain

Your brain is constantly monitoring and fine-tuning what is going on in your body—24 hours a day, year after year—without you even being aware of it.

Answer on page 272.

Star Power

LOGIC PLANNING

Fill in each of the empty squares in the grid so that
each star is surrounded by the numbers 1 through 8
with no repeats.

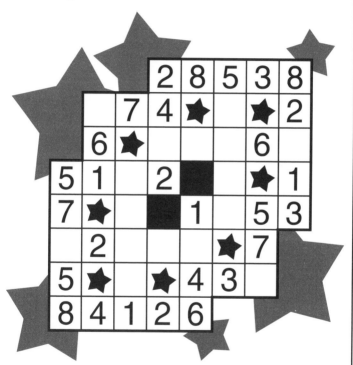

LOGIC

ANALYSIS

Eavesdropping Logic

You have overheard the following comment about a situation between some friends. From this passage, what information can you gather?

"Sergio and Matthew looked grieved to hear the news, but Matthew was distracted by the prospect of related issues. Simone misinterpreted Matthew's attitude and was, frankly, annoyed."

A. Simone dislikes Matthew.

B. Matthew has more pressing concerns.

C. Simone is a bad judge of character.

D. There is no option among the 3 above that fits.

LOGIC

COMPUTATION

Go Figure

Fill each square in the grid with a number from 1 through 4. The numbers in each row must multiply to the totals in the right-hand column. The numbers in each column must multiply to the totals on the bottom line. The numbers in each diagonal must multiply to the totals in the upper and lower right corners.

				20
4	5	3	2	240
3	3	5	5	225
3	1		4	96
2	5	4	1	120
3	4	2	2	48

12 216 300 480 80   48

Answers on page 272.

At the Movies

Each row of moviegoers (horizontal, diagonal, and vertical) has one thing in common. Can you find it before the final credits roll?

ABCD

Place the letter A, B, C, or D in each empty square of the grid. The tables above and to the left indicate how many times each letter appears in that column or row. No letter can be horizontally or vertically adjacent to itself.

				A	1	2	1	3	0	2
				B	2	2	2	0	2	1
				C	3	0	1	2	2	1
A	B	C	D	0	2	2	1	2	2
3	1	1	1						
2	0	2	2						D
0	3	1	2						
3	0	2	1						
0	3	1	2						
1	2	2	1					D	

☼ Trivia on the Brain

Some foods that contain choline—such as soy, peanuts, and eggs—may improve alertness and memory while relieving stress and fatigue. Choline builds the neurotransmitters that pass electrical impulses between brain cells.

Answer on page 273.

You Are Here

...and the taxi meter is ticking. This professional building is a maze of corridors and cubicles. Elevators are local or express only; there are no stairs. And over-stressed office workers won't give you directions to the exit. Why, oh why, did you ever come in here? Doesn't matter now—time to get moving!

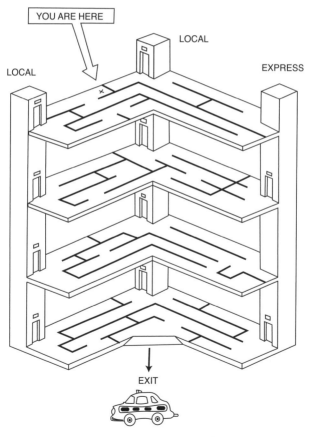

Answer on page 273. **181**

Logidoku

The numbers 1 through 9 appear once in every row, column, long diagonal, irregular shape, and 3 by 3 grid. From the numbers given, can you complete the puzzle?

3		9		8				
			2					
						8		3
							1	
5				1				9
			7		4			
		6						
					4			

Missing Someone?

Among A through D, which is the missing number?

17 14 8 23 15 16 12 __ 26 5

A. 0

B. 5

C. 19

D. 101

Answers on page 273.

Cube Quandary

This is the same cube from 4 different perspectives.
How would the faces appear if the cube were unfolded?

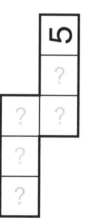

Trivia on the Brain

A piece of a human brain about the size of a grain of sand contains 100,000 neurons and 1 billion synapses, all "talking" to one another.

Answer on page 273.

Cheap Tickets

Across

1. Popular breakfast restaurant (abbr.)
5. Kind of test
9. Not many
12. Conference _____
13. Sharp implements
14. Homer's H
15. Ballpark benches
18. Freebie seeker
19. Moved slowly to the top
20. Have a hamburger
22. One _____ time
23. Sea bordered by Yemen
27. Baseball commissioner Selig
30. Theater section
34. Popular
35. Song written by Queen Lili'uokalani
36. Paranormal ability
39. Fictional news show on "Murphy Brown"
40. From long ago
44. Phytoplankton. e.g.
48. Kids' area on "The Howdy Doody Show"
50. Spoiled
51. It may explode when split
52. Canal between Albany and Buffalo

53. Place for a facial
54. Pear variety
55. Check one's e-mail, say

Down

1. Minutemen, for one: abbr.
2. Video game saga of Master Chief
3. Pancake topper
4. Sugar pill, sometimes
5. Derisive cry
6. Corp. muckety-muck
7. _____ cotta
8. Plus
9. Accomplishment
10. Rebuke to Brutus
11. Bald-faced hornet, actually
16. Part of a bicycle mechanism
17. Air-quality org.
21. Son of Abe Lincoln
23. Volcanic deposit
24. Old carmaker

25. Do something
26. Yao Ming's org.
27. Feathery scarf
28. Popular card game
29. Pre-Easter purchase
31. Former presidential candidate Landon
32. Dedicated
33. Story about monsters
36. Richard Strauss's "_____ wollt ein Sträusslein binden"

37. Fancy menu bird
38. _____ the test
40. Manhunt announcements: abbr.
41. Kind of tide
42. Showoff's exclamation
43. They may clash
45. "American Gigolo" star
46. Operatic number
47. Looked at
49. "Mad Men" network

Crypto-Logic

Each of the numbers in the sequence below represents a letter. Use the mathematical clues to determine which number stands for which letter, and then reveal the encrypted word.

Hint: Remember that the sign / indicates "divided by" and that all sums in parentheses must be done first.

$$7\ 3\ 2\ 9\ 1\ 3\ 2\ 4\ 7$$

Clues: The combined value of all the instances of the numbers that repeat in this encryption is equal to the value of $(Q + 14)$.

$Q = D + S + 1$

$2D = Q + E$

$S = \frac{1}{5}\ Q$

The repeated number you still don't know represents I.

I squared equals G.

$Q - G = U$

Animal Sounds

When read a certain way, which one of the following is not a bird or an animal?

B80	GO80	R80
C80	H80	STO80

Answers on pages 273–274.

Cross-Math

COMPUTATION PLANNING

Place the digits 1 through 9 in the empty white squares so that the 3 horizontal and 3 vertical equations are true. Each digit will be used exactly once. Calculations are done from left to right and from top to bottom.

	+		-		=	6
+		-		+		
	×		-		=	2
+		+		÷		
	÷		+		=	10
=		=		=		
10		6		2		

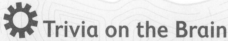

Trivia on the Brain
The brain of a goldfish makes up 0.3 percent of its total body weight. An adult human brain is about 2 percent of the body's total weight.

LANGUAGE

CREATIVE THINKING

Between the Lines

Solve for the middle (undefined) word in each 3-word set. For each set, all 3 words appear on the same page in the dictionary in the order they are given. Rearrange the middle words to complete a quote from Ralph Waldo Emerson.

Example: putter: to work at random; tinker
puzzle
pygmy: one of a race of dwarfs

_ _ _ _ _ _ _ _ _: to show hospitality
_ _ t h _ _ _ _ _ _
_ _ _ _ _ _: tempt by offering pleasure

_ _ _ _: a dull, persistent pain
_ _ _ _ _ _ _ _
_ _ _ _ l l _ _: the greatest warrior among the
Greeks at Troy

_ _ _ _ _ _: rendered animal fat
_ _ _ _ _
_ _ e e _: a selfish and excessive desire for more of
something

_ _ _ _: to record or preserve in writing
_ _ t h _ _ _
_ _ _ _ _ _: become aware of

" _ _ _ _ _ _ _   _ _ _ _ _ _ _ was ever _ _ _ _ _ _(d) without _ _ _ _ _ _ _."

Answers on page 274.

Name Calling

Decipher the encoded words in the quip below using the numbers and letters on the phone pad. Each number can stand for 3 or 4 possible letters.

ANALYSIS

1	2 ABC	3 DEF
4 GHI	5 JKL	6 MNO
7 PQRS	8 TUV	9 WXYZ
	0	

When 5–8–2–5 joins in the 4–2–6–3, 2–5–3–8–3–7–6–3–7–7 scores 3–6–8–2–5–3.

Name Game (Part I)

MEMORY

Study the 9 pairs of names below for 3 minutes. Mentally link each pair as shown, and then turn the page for a memory challenge.

GEORGINA	MATTHEW	HEATHER
HOWARD	JANE	DAVID
CAROL	ANGELA	JONATHAN
GORDON	JAMIE	STEPHANIE
DAVINA	PETER	TOM
ROBERT	CAROLINE	DOROTHY

Answer on page 274.

MEMORY

Name Game (Part II)

(Don't read this page until you've read page 189!)

Based on what you recall from the previous page, draw a line that connects each name to its original partner.

ANGELA	ROBERT
JONATHAN	JAMIE
GEORGINA	GORDON
DAVINA	CAROLINE
TOM	DAVID
CAROL	DOROTHY
MATTHEW	STEPHANIE
PETER	HOWARD
HEATHER	JANE

Vex-a-Gon

PLANNING

Place the numbers 1 through 6 into the triangles of each hexagon. The numbers may be in any order, but they do not repeat within each hexagon shape.

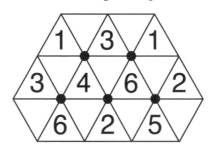

CREATIVE THINKING

190

Answers on page 274.

Hashi

Each circle represents an island, with the number inside indicating the number of bridges connected to it. Draw bridges between islands using the number given, but there can be no more than 2 bridges going in the same direction, and there must be a continuous path connecting all islands. Bridges can be only vertical or horizontal and may not cross islands or other bridges.

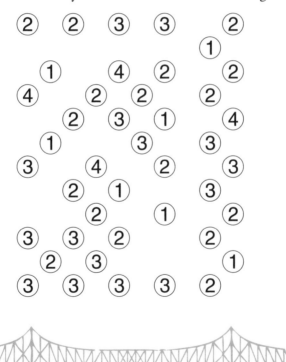

PLANNING

LOGIC

Logidoku

Place the numbers 1 through 9 once in every row, column, long diagonal, irregular shape, and 3 by 3 grid. With the numbers given, complete the puzzle.

						1		
7							2	
				8				
6		1						
	3			5		4		
					2			
		2		8			7	
4								6

LOGIC

Eleven Coins

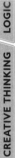

Among 11 coins of the same denomination, 1 is known to be counterfeit. Using a simple 2-pan scale, or balance, how would you determine in 2 weighings if the fake is heavier or lighter than a real coin?

CREATIVE THINKING

192

Answers on pages 274–275.

Cross Count

In the chart below, all the letters of the alphabet have been given a value between 1 and 9. Using the chart, fill in the squares to create 4-letter words that add up to the numbers at the end of the rows and below the columns.

1	2	3	4	5	6	7	8	9
A	B	C	D	E	F	G	H	I
J	K	L	M	N	O	P	Q	R
S	T	U	V	W	X	Y	Z	

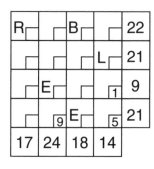

Rhyme Time

Each clue leads to a 2-word answer that rhymes, such as BIG PIG or STABLE TABLE. The numbers in parentheses after the clue give the number of letters in each word.

1. Talent with a tool (5, 5): _____

2. Arrive at last at the seashore (5, 5): _____

3. Blamed the trouble on a type of shake (7, 6): _____

4. Bother the court entertainer (6, 6): _____

5. Obsession with re-invasion (12, 13): _____

PLANNING

LANGUAGE

Word Columns

Find the hidden quote by using the letters directly below each of the blank squares. Each letter is used only once. A black square indicates the end of a word.

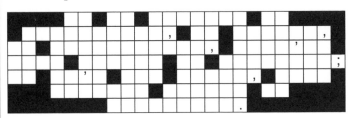

```
          i            e
       k e n l    t o      o     y
   i t a s t a d t   a h c n u   i t
 a   p r e c p e v g m v i r l t   i s   e
o r   t l m p p n n e r r d i t g h e r r o y
s t t s n o x a e l s e i k r e e m e t h l l
i f o i t f a y i s a i t t a y e s o f u l w
```

VISUAL SEARCH

How Many Rectangles?

How many rectangles of any size are formed by the lines in this figure? Do not include any squares in your count.

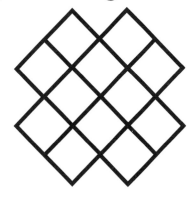

ATTENTION

Answers on page 275.

Word Ladder

Use the clues to change just one letter on each line to go from the top word to the bottom word. Do not change the order of the letters. You must have a common English word at each step.

FOLKY

_____   naïve idiocy

_____   Christmas plant

_____   Swiss cheese

_____   Winnie the Pooh loves it

_____   makes the world go round

MONET

Digital Sudoku

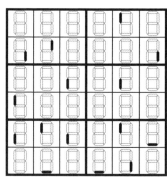

Fill in the grid so that each row, column, and 2 by 3 box contains the numbers 1 through 6 exactly once. Numbers are in digital form. Some segments have been filled in.

PLANNING | SPATIAL REASONING

For Intrepid Hikers

It may be just a walk in the park, but this maze will take you around a few turns and into many dead ends.

S

F

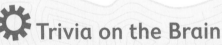

☼ Trivia on the Brain

Believe it or not, thinking takes energy. More blood flows to the brain when we think hard, and that takes energy from elsewhere in our bodies.

Answer on page 275.

Kakuro

Place a number from 1 through 9 in each empty cell so that the sum of each vertical or horizontal run (rows and columns extending from already numbered cells) equals the number at the top or on the left of that run. Numbers may not be repeated in any run, and runs end at dark-colored squares.

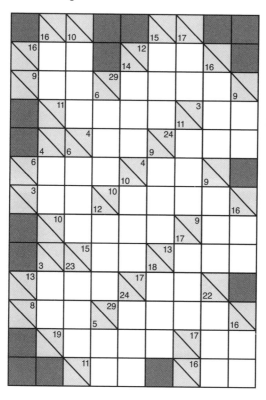

PROBLEM SOLVING

LOGIC

Cast-a-Word

There are 4 dice, and there are different letters of the alphabet on the 6 faces of each of them (each letter appears only once). Random throws of the dice produced the words in this list. Can you figure out which letters appear on each of the 4 dice?

BACK	GAVE	JUMP	SKIT
BAND	GRID	PLAY	VEST
FOWL	HOLE	QUAY	
FUSE	JACK	SANE	

CREATIVE THINKING

Classical Sequence

Identify the missing letter (it represents a musical composition).

G G G ___ F F F D

ANALYSIS

198

Grid Fill

To complete this puzzle, place the given letters and words into the shapes in this grid. Words and letters will run across, down, and wrap around each shape. When the grid is filled, each row will contain one of the following words: amount, dances, Darwin, kettle, Monday, sprall, sugars.

1. D, L, S, T

2. NT, PR

3. RUG, SIN

4. DATA, WARS, YELL

5. OUNCE, SMOKE

6. AMANDA

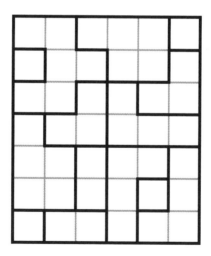

Greenback Ovals

Fill in the blank spaces as you would in a crossword puzzle. The theme—or title—of the puzzle might seem ambiguous, but it should suggest a category of words that when linked together will complete the puzzle.

For example: HOLE IN ONE might suggest DOUGHNUTS. Or, it might suggest GOLF, which would lead to the words CLUB, IRON, TEE, etc., all linked by a common theme. Notice that a few letters are already in place, and some of the words intersect, which adds to the mystery, and the fun, of finding the solution.

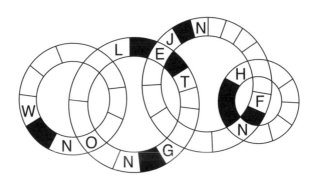

 Trivia on the Brain

Dates, statistics, and other factual memories (such as trivia) are stored in the front left side of the brain.

Answer on page 276.

Movie Title and Director Cryptogram

Cryptograms are messages in code. Break the code below to reveal 4 films and their directors. For example, THE SMART CAT might become FVO QWGDF JGF if **F** is substituted for **T, V** for **H, O** for **E,** and so on.

1. KMABL SJ KMABLFTIB:
   EPWATR LNBOLOMOV

2. BLT ILNKNKD: IBEKPTJ
   VGSANOV

3. ONBNQTK VEKT: MAIMK
   FTPPTI

4. AEDNKD SGPP: XEABNK
   IOMAITIT

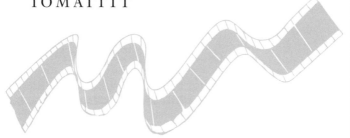

PLANNING

LOGIC

1-2-3

Place the numbers 1, 2, and 3 in the circles below. The challenge is to have only these 3 numbers in each connected row or column—no number should repeat. Any combination is allowed.

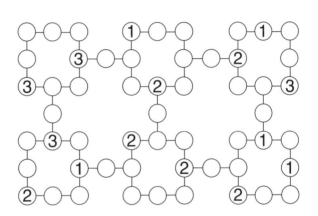

LOGIC

Sudoku

Use deductive logic to complete the grid so that each row, column, and 3 by 3 box contains the numbers 1 through 9 in some order. The solution is unique.

			8				9	
				6				
5	7					6		1
		2	7				5	
	1	6		9		3	8	
	3				2	9		
2		3					4	5
				7				
	5				3			

Answers on page 276.

Rating the Guys

According to the dating service's new rating system, Buddy and Freddy are 6's, Bob and Ned are 3's, and Jonathan is a 9. What is Antonio?

Fitting Words

In this miniature crossword, the clues are listed randomly and are numbered for convenience only. It is up to you to figure out the placement of the 9 answers. To help you, we've inserted the letter **I** in the grid, and this is the only occurrence of that letter in the puzzle.

1. Odometer reading
2. Patella site
3. Door frame upright
4. Queens' inferiors
5. Guff

6. Barn bundles
7. Battery
8. Opera solo
9. Large stadium

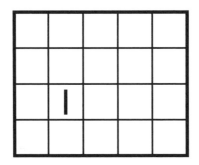

As a Formality

Across

1. Compact item?
5. Point de Gaze, for one
9. "To Wong _____, Thanks for Everything, Julie Newmar"
12. Harvard rival
13. Julia's Oscar-winning role
14. Musical actress Salonga
15. "Godfrey Daniels!"
16. Creature with a long tongue
18. Formal fight?
20. Tried partner
21. Business magazine
22. Body-shop figure
24. Charlton Heston was its pres.
26. From the top
30. Formal falderal?
34. Crime boss
35. Trophy form
36. Microscopic
37. Short-billed songbird
40. Brewed beverages
42. Formal vehicle?
46. Kind of invoice
48. Fabled racer
49. Chit
50. Fraulein's refusal
51. Fleecy females

52. S. E. Hinton novel
53. Hunt for
54. Card game with a 32-card deck

Down

1. Changed the color of
2. Venetian villain
3. Desk feature, sometimes
4. Lebanon symbol
5. G8 summit meeting attendees
6. Kuwaiti, e.g.
7. Botanical tendrils
8. Conclude with
9. Criticism
10. "The Strife is _____, the Battle Done" (hymn)
11. Bucket material
17. Word in many Grammy categories

19. Pioneering Soviet spacecraft series
22. Mail Boxes _____
23. _____ Na Na
25. Pro Bowl side
27. Scoop searcher
28. Palindromic preposition
29. Zed predecessor
31. Wallpaper design
32. Have more stripes, say

33. Newspaper page
38. Clickable pictures
39. Outside hoops shot
41. Fire remnants
42. Cajun-cooking thickener
43. Philippe's steady
44. Zone
45. "Batman" star
46. Racetrack station
47. "Dizzy" singer Tommy

1	2	3	4		5	6	7	8		9	10	11
12					13					14		
15					16				17			
18				19								
	20					21					
22	23			24		25			26	27	28	29
30			31				32	33				
34						35				36		
		37	38	39		40		41			
	42				43					44	45
46	47							48			
49				50				51			
52				53				54			

Answers on page 277. **205**

ANALYSIS | COMPUTATION

Lunch Plans

Between 2,200 and 2,600 guests were invited to the mayor's luncheon. The organizer decided to arrange the seating so that each table would accommodate an equal number of guests, and the number of guests at each table would be an odd number.

The organizer determined that the following arrangements would not work:
3 guests per table (2 would be left without seating);
5 guests per table (4 left out); 7 guests per table (6 left out); and 9 guests per table (8 left out).

However, when he tried seating 11 guests per table, no guests were left without a place to sit.

How many guests in total were invited to the luncheon?

LANGUAGE | PLANNING

Word Ladder

Use the clues to change just one letter on each line to go from the top word to the bottom word. Do not change the order of the letters. You must have a common English word at each step.

CLOUD

_____ a serious punch

_____ to pointedly break rules

_____ if less dense than water

_____ express malicious pleasure

_____ a thick Medieval coin

GREAT

Answers on page 277.

Perfect Score

Make 3 successful hits so that the sum of the numbers is 100. Double and triple scores do not apply. Numbers may be used more than once.

⚙ Trivia on the Brain

Just as the body benefits from activities such as sit-ups and swimming, the brain builds its muscles through a variety of mental activities. There is growing evidence that people who engage in puzzles, board games, and other mentally stimulating activities can reduce the risk of memory loss and dementia as they age.

Answer on page 277.

Clone It!

Use the grid dots as a guide to split the shaded shape into 2 smaller shapes that are either identical or mirror each other.

For a hint, study the example illustrations below.

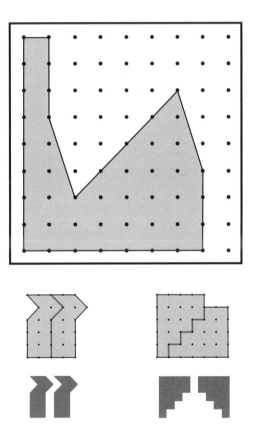

Answer on page 277.

Between the Lines

Solve for the middle (undefined) words in each 3-word set. For each set, all 3 words appear on the same page in the dictionary in the order they are given. Rearrange the middle words to complete a quote from Titus Plautus.

Example: putter: to work at random; tinker
puzzle
pygmy: one of a race of dwarfs

_ _ _ _ _ _: voucher for a discount on a particular product

_ _ _ _ _ _ _

_ _ _ _ _ _: route or direction followed by a ship

_ _ _ _ _ _ _: a cell in which chemical energy is converted to electricity

_ _ _ _ _ _

_ _ _ _: weep or cry noisily

_ _ _ _: free from defect, disease, or infirmity

_ _ _ f

_ _ _ _: a corridor

_ _ _ _: a native or national of Denmark

_ _ _ _ _ _

_ _ _ _ _ _: to hang loosely and be able to swing freely

"_____ in _____ is _____ the _____."

PLANNING

LOGIC

Logidoku

The numbers 1 through 9 should appear once in every row, column, long diagonal, irregular shape, and 3 by 3 grid. With the numbers given, complete the puzzle.

		8				4		
7			3				1	
						6		
								2
					5			
	4							
						2		8
			6				9	
8					9			

Wacky Wordy

Can you "read" the phrase below?

LANGUAGE

ANALYSIS

HIT

DER

210

Answers on page 277.

Alien Mutations

Shown are 16 mutation chambers surrounded by alien figures. Each of the 4 aliens on the left passed through the 4 chambers to the right and was transformed on the other side (e.g., the alien on the left of A passed through chambers A, B, C, and D and mutated into the alien to the right of D). The same is true for the aliens above the chambers. Each one passed through the 4 chambers directly below them and then came out mutated on the other side.

Each chamber effects one—and only one—alteration (changes in head or body shape, changes in posture, addition/removal of appendages).

What mutation is each chamber responsible for?

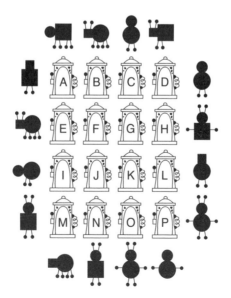

Paint-by-Number

Bud and Lou had to paint a fence that ran along each side of a street. Bud arrived first and painted 3 yards of fencing on the right side. When Lou arrived, he pointed out that Bud should be painting the left side. So Bud started on the left side, and Lou continued what Bud had started on the right side.

When Lou finished his side, he crossed the street and painted 6 yards of fencing for Bud, which completed the job. Both sides of the street had an equal length and height of fencing.

Who painted the greatest length of fencing, and by how much?

Vex-a-Gon

Place the numbers 1 through 6 into the triangles of each hexagon. The numbers may be in any order, but they do not repeat within each hexagon shape.

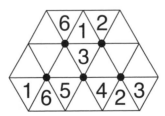

Answers on page 278.

Identity Parade

Oops! Four mug shots were accidentally sent through the shredder, and Officer Barry is trying to straighten them out. Currently, only one facial feature in each row is in its correct place. Officer Barry knows that:

1. C's eyes are 1 place to the left of his mouth.
2. B's mouth is not next to C's mouth.
3. A's nose is 1 place to the left of D's hair.
4. B's eyes are on the same face as A's mouth and are 1 place to the right of B's hair.
5. B's nose is 1 place to the right of his mouth.

Can you find the correct hair, eyes, nose, and mouth for each person?

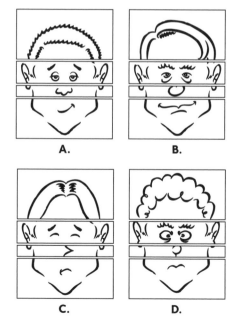

A.　　　　**B.**

C.　　　　**D.**

LANGUAGE PLANNING

Word Ladder

Change just one letter on each line to go from the top word to the bottom word. Do not change the order of the letters. You must have a common English word at each step.

FISH

_____

_____

_____

_____

_____

_____

HOOK

COMPUTATION PLANNING

Cross-Math

Place the digits 1 through 9 in the empty white squares so that the 3 horizontal and 3 vertical equations are true. Each digit will be used exactly once. Calculations are done from left to right and from top to bottom.

	+		-		=	8
÷		+		+		
	×		÷		=	2
-		-		+		
	×		-		=	5
=		=		=		
3		7		16		

Answers on page 278.

ABCD

Every cell in this grid contains one of 4 letters: A, B, C, or D. No letter can be horizontally or vertically adjacent to itself. The tables above and to the left of the grid indicate how many times each letter appears in that column or row.

Can you complete the grid?

		A	2	3	1	1	1	1	1	1	2
		B	3	2	1	2	1	2	2	2	1
		C	0	1	1	2	1	2	1	2	1
A B C	D	1	0	3	1	3	1	2	1	2
2 0 4 3										
2 5 0 2										
0 4 3 2										
4 1 2 2										
4 2 2 1										
1 4 0 4										

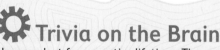

🌟 Trivia on the Brain

Neurons last for an entire lifetime. They are among the oldest cells in the human body.

Fit It

Use each of the words, names, and acronyms found below to complete the clueless crossword grid on the next page. The puzzle has only one solution.

3 letters
AGO
ALE
ATM
BAT
CPU
ELI
ETE
NOG
OAR
REP
RIP
SNL
TAP
TEA
TIC
TOT

4 letters
ARTS
BREW
ONTO
ORES
REDO
TARE

TUNE
WASP

5 letters
ABIDE
ALLOT
CODES
OILER
ORATE
PESOS
ROMAN
SCADS
SEDAN
SIRED
STILE
TATER

6 letters
ALPINE
ATTILA
CACHED
COSTAR
DARTED
EMENDS
LASSIE
ORIOLE

PAPERS
SEALED
SIDLES
SLURPS

7 letters
DESIRES
ENPLANE
HIRE OUT
MORALES
NBA GAME
ORIGAMI
REPOSED

8 letters
CASTANET
MATTRESS

13 letters
MORTGAGE
RATES

Common Sense

Can you determine the missing letter?

S S __ T T

ANALYSIS | CREATIVE THINKING

Elevator Words

Like an elevator, words move up and down the "floors" of this puzzle. Starting with the first answer, the second word from each answer carries down to become the first word of the following answer. With the clues given, complete the puzzle.

Clues
1. This may be used to get the band started
2. Don Quixote–like vision
3. They're simply the best
4. Collective desire to win
5. Adhesive used to attach false hair to skin
6. Substance obtained from acacia trees
7. One of several that appear with this puzzle

1. pitch _____

2. _____ _____

3. _____ _____

4. _____ _____

5. _____ _____

6. _____ _____

7. _____ numeral

218

Answers on page 279.

Say What?

Below are a group of words that, when properly arranged in the blanks, reveal a quote from Ralph Waldo Emerson.

heard   Always   high   young   to   what
counsel   are   I   do   given

"It was _____ _____ that _____ had once _____

_____ _____ a _____ person, '_____ do _____

you _____ afraid to _____.'"

Courier Confusion (Part I)

Sawyer has a letter to deliver but can't remember all the details. Study the fictitious address below for 2 minutes and then turn the page to help him fill in the blanks.

Don Jensen,

The Willows,

4th Floor,

94 Grand Oaks Avenue,

Bakersfield,

Connecticut,

CA 10016

MEMORY

Courier Confusion (Part II)

(Don't read this page until you've read page 219!)

Help Sawyer by filling in the missing information.

Don _____,

The _____,

_____th Floor,

94 _____ Oaks _____,

Bakersfield,

_____,

CA _____

PLANNING

LOGIC

Star Power

Fill each of the empty squares in the grid so that each star is surrounded by the numbers 1 through 8 with no repeats.

Answers on page 279.

Digital Sudoku

Fill in the grid so that each row, column, and 2 by 3 box contains the numbers 1 through 6 exactly once. Numbers are in digital form, and some segments have been filled in.

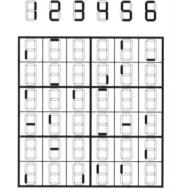

LOGIC

A Shapely Challenge

How many quadrilateral shapes (those with 4 sides) are in this mind-boggling puzzle?

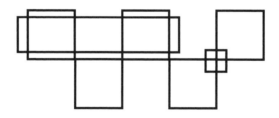

CREATIVE THINKING   SPATIAL VISUALIZATION   VISUAL LOGIC

Won't You Join Us?

Every word listed below is contained within the group of letters on the next page. They can be found in a straight line horizontally, vertically, or diagonally and may read either backward or forward. Each word can join with another word to form a new word. For example, if the list contained JIG and SAW, they can form JIGSAW. Can you put all these together?

ARROW	FEATHER
BACK	FILE
BAG	FLOWER
BAND	FLY
BARN	GROUND
BAT	HEAD
BED	LADY
BIRD	MOBILE
BLOCK	NAIL
BOOK	NEWS
BOX	PIG
BREAK	PIPE
BRICK	POT
BROW	SAND
BUCK	SKIN
BUG	STAND
BULL	STONE
BUSTER	STORM
BUTTER	TACK
CAT	TAIL
CLOCK	THUMB
CORNER	TIME
DOG	WAGON
EYE	WEIGHT
FAST	WORK

```
D L T F F X G E G K G
  F L O W E R I K D
  Q K E N O T S
    F D P U N
      W I N
      O P D
      R E P
      B A L
      A R G
      C R I
      K O R
    Y C W M R
    L H A R O Q N
  F E A T H E R I F
  G A B L D O G T K B D
  R D S C U I Y B C S F R X
  R E T T U B B B O T W U I E G
N M N A A Z R A L O D E E B L A Y
P I A R I B K I C R D M N O I M E K T
T I K O L T A C M B N D X A O G U Y B
L O G C B O O K O W A G O N T K H H E
N H U Y U J T P R L S N K Q U S I T T
  M B S X B U L L A B S D G R J X F
```

LOGIC

Class Schedule

Fred has lost his school schedule and, in trying to recall it, has made errors in the order he must attend his classes. Although each item is in the correct column, only one item in each column is correctly positioned.

The following facts are true about the correct positions:
1. Neither Art nor Kettering is sixth.
2. Room D5 is 2 places below Harrison and 1 above Biology.
3. Jones is not in room E9 and is not directly above or below Irving in the list.
4. Room B1 is 3 places below Jones and 2 below English.
5. Room A2 is 1 place below Irving and 1 above Chemistry.

Can you find the correct subject, teacher, and room for each class in the schedule?

	Subject	Teacher	Room
1	Art	Gates	A2
2	Biology	Harrison	B1
3	Chemistry	Irving	C8
4	History	Jones	D5
5	English	Kettering	E9
6	Geography	Lee	F7

Answers on page 279.

Codeword

Each letter of the alphabet is hidden in code and is represented by a random number from 1 through 26. With the letter given, break the code by completing the crossword with common English words.

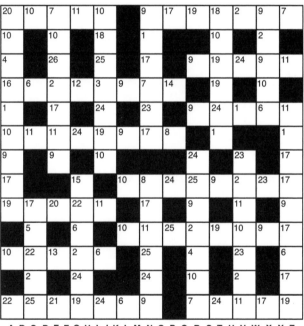

| A B C D E F G H I J K L M N O P Q R S T U V W X Y Z |

1	2	3	4	5	6	7	8	9	10	11	12	13

14	15	16	17	18	19	20	21	22	23	24	25	26
	J											

LOGIC

ANALYSIS

Fences

Connect the dots and draw a continuous path that doesn't cross itself. Numbers represent the "fences" created by the path (2 edges are created around the number 2, 3 edges around 3, etc.). We've started the puzzle for you.

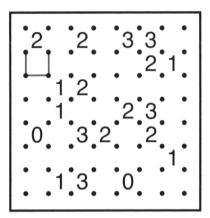

VISUAL LOGIC

Concise Concept

Based on simple design, which figure is the odd one out?

SPATIAL VISUALIZATION

1.   **2.**   **3.**   **4.**   **5.**

CREATIVE THINKING

Answers on page 280.

Kakuro

Place a number from 1 through 9 in each empty cell so that the sum of each vertical or horizontal run (rows and columns extending from already numbered cells) equals the number at the top or on the left of that run. Numbers may not be repeated in any run, and runs end at dark-colored squares.

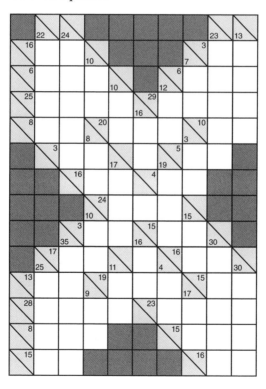

Crypto-Logic

Each of the numbers in the sequence below represents a letter. Use the mathematical clues to determine which number stands for which letter in order to reveal the encrypted word. There are more clues than you'll need.

1 4 7 1 6 8 9 6 3

Clues

N is the fourth prime.
A is a double square.
D is spatial.
Twelve U's in an hour.
O is quadrilateral.
C is unity.

L is the first non-prime odd one (other than C).
E is the best when it comes to a die.
S is dichotomy.

Go Figure

Fill each square in the grid with a number from 1 through 4. When the numbers in each row are multiplied, you should arrive at the total in the right-hand column. When the numbers in each column are multiplied, you should arrive at the total on the bottom line. The

864

	3	4	4	2	5	1	960
4		5	1	1	3	4	480
3	1	3		2	4		432
3	4	2	6		1	2	1152
	3	4	3	3		5	3240
5	2	3	4	1	2		720
	6		1	4	3	2	864

2160 864 2880 576 192 1080 720   864

numbers in each long diagonal must multiply to the totals in the upper and lower right corners.

Answers on page 280.

Number Crossword

Fill in this crossword with numbers instead of letters.
Use the clues to determine which of the numbers
1 through 9 belongs in each square. No zeros are used.

Across
1. An even number
3. An even number in the
   form ABAB
5. 3-Across plus 4-Down
6. An even number

Down
1. Its last digit is the sum of
   its first 2 digits
2. Its last digit is the product
   of its first 2 digits
3. Three identical digits
4. A square number

		1	2
3	4		
5			
6			

Vex-a-Gon

Place the numbers 1 through 6 into the triangles of each
hexagon. The numbers may be in any order, but they do
not repeat within each hexagon shape.

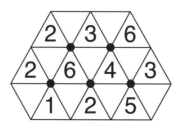

Supermarket Shenanigans

Checkout Charlie was convinced he was being cheated by the automated checkout scanner at the grocery store, so he memorized the prices of every item in the supermarket, then watched the screen as the clerk scanned the items of every customer in front of him. The man in the green shirt had a jar of applesauce and
a pound of beef, which scanned correctly for a total of $5.40. The woman with the red scarf had a bag of candy and a doughnut, which scanned correctly for a total of $2.90. The man in blue shorts had a pound of beef and a carton of eggnog, which scanned correctly for a total of $7.10. The woman in the pink skirt had a doughnut and a jar of applesauce, which scanned correctly for a total of $3.10. The man with the purple cap had a carton of eggnog and a bag of candy, which scanned correctly for a total of $5.70. When it was Checkout Charlie's turn, he was distracted by the attractive checkout clerk, who was wearing a multicolored top. She told him his total was $4.80, and Charlie paid without ever taking his eyes off her, so he didn't check that his two items had scanned correctly. Because he bought two items that had already been scanned, the total was correct. Which two items did love-struck Charlie buy, and how much did each of the scanned items cost?

Answers on page 281.

Logidoku

Place the numbers 1 through 9 once in every row, column, long diagonal, irregular shape, and 3 by 3 grid. From the numbers given, can you complete the puzzle?

⚙ Trivia on the Brain

If you continue to learn and challenge yourself throughout your life, your brain continues to grow! An active brain produces new dendrites, which are the connections between nerve cells that allow them to communicate with one another. This helps the brain store and retrieve information more easily.

Pharmacy Fountain

The object is to fill in the blank spaces as you would a crossword puzzle. The theme—or title—of the puzzle might appear to be ambiguous, but it should suggest a category of words that, when linked together, will complete the puzzle.

For example: HOLE IN ONE might suggest DOUGHNUTS. Or it might suggest GOLF, which would lead to the words CLUB, IRON, TEE, etc., all linked by a common theme. Notice that a few letters are already in place, and some of the words intersect—which adds to the mystery, and the fun, of finding the solution.

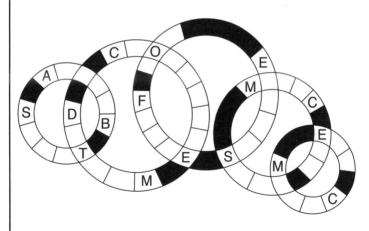

Answer on page 281.

Hashi

Each circle shown here represents an island, with the number inside indicating how many bridges are connected to that island. Based on those numbers, draw bridges between islands so that there is a continuous path connecting all the islands but no more than 2 bridges between any 2 islands. Bridges can be only horizontal or vertical and may not cross over islands or other bridges.

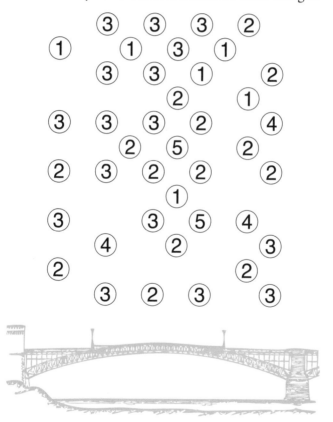

PLANNING

LOGIC

Mathematics Letterbox

The letters in CUBE can be found in boxes 2, 4, 9, and 24, but not necessarily in that order. Similarly, the letters in all the other mathematical terms below can be found in the boxes indicated. Insert all the letters of the alphabet into the boxes; if you do this correctly, the shaded cells will reveal another math term.

Hint: Look for words that share a single letter. For example, CUBOID shares a **D** with PYRAMID and a **U** with SQUARE. By comparing the number lists, you can then deduce the values of these letters.

AXIS: 12, 15, 19, 20
CIRCLE: 2, 18, 19, 23, 24
CUBE: 2, 4, 9, 24
CUBOID: 2, 4, 9, 13, 19, 26
FIGURE: 9, 18, 19, 22, 24, 25
KITE: 8, 17, 19, 24
POLYGON: 3, 13, 14, 21, 22, 23
POWER: 10, 13, 14, 18, 24
PYRAMID: 3, 11, 14, 18, 19, 20, 26
RHOMBUS: 4, 6, 9, 11, 13, 15, 18
SPHERE: 6, 14, 15, 18, 24
SQUARE: 5, 9, 15, 18, 20, 24
TRAPEZIUM: 7, 9, 11, 14, 17, 18, 19, 20, 24
VECTOR: 2, 13, 16, 17, 18, 24

1	2	3	4	5	6	7	8	9	10	11	12	13
J												

14	15	16	17	18	19	20	21	22	23	24	25	26

Answer on page 281.

Cross Sums

Use the numbers below to fill in the grid. Each cell at the top of a cross is the sum of numbers below it. So, as seen in the example, A = B + C + D + E.

1 3 4 5 6 7 8 9 10 11 12 30 43 47 57

64 98 121 177 386 431 439 1433

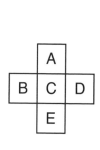

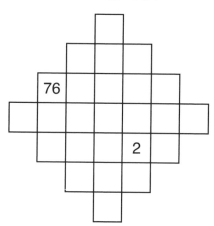

Trivia on the Brain

The first crossword puzzle was called a "word-cross" and looked very different from most cross-words of today: It had no black squares and was in the shape of a diamond.

LOGIC

ANALYSIS

Flip the Cards

Three cards have been laid out, each marked with a letter on one side and a number on the other. If you want to make sure that every card with a 4 has an **S** on the other side and that cards with a 7 have an **F** on the other side, which cards need to be turned over?

A. All 3 cards

B. The card on the left and the card on the right

C. The card on the right and the card in the middle

D. The card on the left and the card in the middle

LOGIC

Sudoku

Use deductive logic to complete the grid so that each row, each column, and each 3 by 3 box contains the numbers 1 through 9 in some order. The solution is unique.

	6	5				7	1	
8					1			
		3		9				
4		1	2					
	2			7			5	
					5	2		3
				8		9		
			6					7
	1	7				3	2	

Answers on pages 281–282.

Sciences Scramblegram

Four 11-letter words, all of which revolve around the same theme, have been jumbled. Unscramble the 4 words and write the answers in the space next to each one. Then transfer the letters in the shaded boxes into the shaded row below and unscramble the 9-letter word that goes with the theme. The theme for this puzzle is sciences.

```
U S E R A I N C O A T

C                      C
A                      O
T                      Y
S                      G
T                      R
A                      I
M                      M
E                      L
H                      I
I                      O
M                      N

      S L I C I N G S U I T
```

LOGIC PLANNING

1-2-3

Place the numbers 1, 2, and 3 in the circles below.
The challenge is to have only these 3 numbers in each
connected row and column—no number should repeat.
Any combination is allowed.

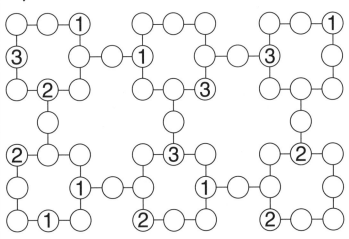

⚙ Trivia on the Brain

The "terrible twos" aren't toddlers in rebellion. At
this point in their lives, their brains have developed
sooner than their ability to express themselves.
When they feel that they can't communicate their
needs, they get frustrated and lash out.

Answer on page 282.

Word Jigsaw

LANGUAGE PLANNING

Fit the puzzle pieces into the frame below to form common, uncapitalized words reading across and down crossword-style. There's no need to rotate the pieces; they'll fit as shown, with each piece used exactly once.

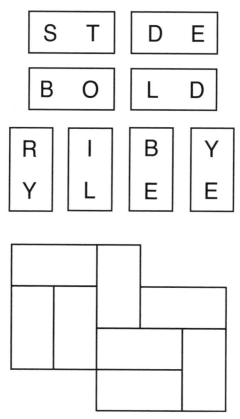

LOGIC

Digital Sudoku

Fill in the grid so that each row, column, and 2 by 3 box contains the numbers 1 through 6 exactly once. Numbers are in digital form, and some segments have been filled in.

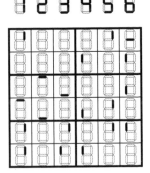

PLANNING

GENERAL KNOWLEDGE

Fitting Words

In this miniature crossword, the clues are listed randomly and are numbered for convenience only. It is up to you to figure out the placement of the 9 answers. To help you, we've inserted one letter in the grid, and this is the only occurrence of that letter in the puzzle.

1. A long time

2. A long, long time

3. Constellation part

4. Precept

5. No longer in port

6. Clear the chalkboard

7. Collect bit by bit

8. Like custard

9. Zest

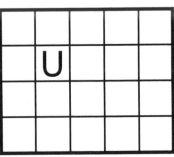

240

Answers on page 282.

Kakuro

Place a number from 1 through 9 in each empty cell so that the sum of each vertical or horizontal run (rows and columns extending from already numbered cells) equals the number at the top or on the left of that run. Numbers may not be repeated in any run, and runs end at dark-colored squares.

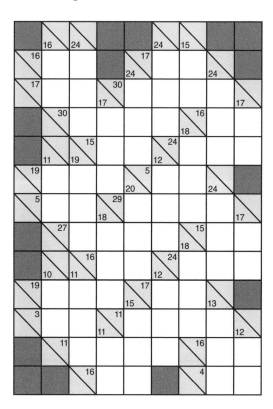

Shakespeare's Women

Every name listed is contained within the group of letters on the next page. They can be found horizontally, vertically, or diagonally and may read either backward or forward. The leftover letters reveal the name of a woman in the life of King Henry IV.

ALICE	HECATE
ANDROMACHE	HERMIONE
ANNE PAGE	IMOGEN
AUDREY	IRAS
BEATRICE	IRIS
CASSANDRA	ISABEL
CELIA	JESSICA
CERES	JOAN
CLEOPATRA	JULIA
CORDELIA	JULIET
CRESSIDA	JUNO
DESDEMONA	
DIANA	
DOLL TEARSHEET	
ELEANOR	
ELIZABETH	
EMILIA	
GONERIL	

242

```
L  A  R  T  A  P  O  E  L  C  L  S  R  M  L
J  U  L  I  E  T  G  A  C  E  D  O  I  A  E
U  T  C  E  T  A  C  E  H  E  N  Y  D  R  L
N  N  E  E  P  E  R  C  Y  A  R  Y  R  I  I
O  P  H  E  L  I  A  O  E  N  M  E  O  N  Z
R  S  N  N  H  M  T  L  L  A  C  H  S  A  A
C  N  A  E  O  S  E  E  C  I  R  T  A  E  B
A  U  D  R  E  Y  R  B  L  R  R  N  L  U  E
S  D  D  I  I  A  E  A  A  A  O  E  I  I  T
S  N  I  S  A  T  I  I  E  M  M  E  N  M  H
A  N  S  S  H  N  L  L  E  T  B  M  E  O  E
N  A  A  A  S  U  A  D  E  R  L  I  L  G  G
D  O  B  G  J  E  S  S  I  C  A  L  A  E  N
R  J  E  D  E  E  R  H  E  R  M  I  O  N  E
A  I  L  E  D  R  O  C  M  I  R  A  N  D  A
```

LADY MACBETH   NERISSA
LUCE   OPHELIA
MARIANA   PERCY (Lady)
MARINA   REGAN
MIRANDA   ROSALINE

Leftover letters spell: _____

_____

LOGIC

ANALYSIS

Battle Boats

Place each ship in the fleet at right within the grid. They may be placed horizontally or vertically, but they can't touch each other (not even diagonally). Numbers reveal the ship segments located in that row or column.

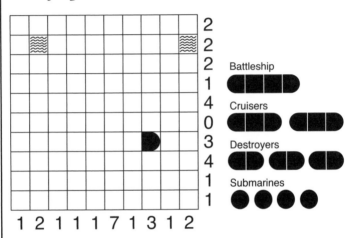

2
2
2
1
4
0
3
4
1
1

1 2 1 1 1 7 1 3 1 2

Battleship

Cruisers

Destroyers

Submarines

PROBLEM SOLVING

Coffee Break

There are 2 empty coffee mugs. One mug holds 3 cups, and the other holds 5 cups. There is also unlimited supply of water and a packet of instant coffee, which when dissolved in 1 cup of water constitutes coffee concentration of 100 percent. Prepare 5 cups that have 12 percent concentration of coffee.

COMPUTATION

Answers on page 283.

Sudoku

Use deductive logic to complete the grid so that each row, column, and 3 by 3 box contains the numbers 1 through 9 in some order. The solution is unique.

6			1	8				
		3				1	6	
			2					8
1		7						
	2		6	1	9		4	
						2		3
8					5			
	9	6				5		
				9	8			2

Vex-a-Gon

Place the numbers 1 through 6 into the triangles of each hexagon. The numbers may be in any order, but they do not repeat within each hexagon shape.

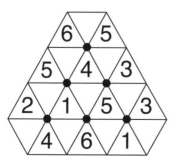

Answers

Vex-a-Gon (page 6)

Word Columns (page 6)

The fellow that owns his own home is always just coming out of a hardware store.

A Puzzling Perspective (page 7)

Grandfather

Liar's Logic (page 7)

The liar is B. A and B contradict, so we know one is lying. Because there are two truth-tellers, C must be telling the truth and, therefore, so must A.

The Great Ape Hunt (pages 8–9)

Leftover letters spell: Alternate titles for the movie were *The Eighth Wonder*, *The Ape*, *King Ape*, *The Beast*, and *Kong*.

World's Easiest Crossword (page 10)

Say What? (page 10)

"The only thing worth living for is the lifting up of our fellow man."

Sudoku (page 11)

2	5	9	6	7	1	4	3	8
7	3	8	2	5	4	9	1	6
1	4	6	8	3	9	2	5	7
4	9	7	5	1	8	3	6	2
8	6	1	7	2	3	5	9	4
5	2	3	9	4	6	8	7	1
6	8	2	1	9	5	7	4	3
9	7	4	3	6	2	1	8	5
3	1	5	4	8	7	6	2	9

Between the Lines (page 12)

wisdom, wise, wish; direct, direction, director; theft, their, them; folk, follow, folly

"The wisest men follow their own direction."

Quic-Kross (page 13)

PEDANT

Alien Mutations (page 14)

A to biped, B add rear appendages, C head circle, D remove antennae, E add front appendages, F body circle, G head square, H to quadraped, I remove front appendages

Cross-Math (page 15)

5	−	2	÷	3	=	1
+		+		×		
9	×	8	−	6	=	66
÷		×		−		
7	−	1	−	4	=	2
=		=		=		
2		10		14		

Wacky Wordy (page 15)

All is fair in love and war.

The Loopy Lexicon
(page 16)

Find the Word (page 17)

CLOVEr LOVEd working at the gLOVE factory, but her dream was to start a soLO VEnture making rolLOVEr bars and covers for convertibles. For lunch, she ate buffaLO, VEgetables, and cheese cooked in a smalL OVEn. Her lunch occasionally had spilLOVEr, so she cleaned the smalL OVEn with BrilLO VEry carefully. CLOVEr's boyfriend, GLOVEr, who worked at the coverall factory, LOVEd the freckles she had alL OVEr her face. The two LOVEbirds dated often but never had sleepovers. GLOVEr longed to be a portobelLO VEndor but instead went to night school to study piccoLO, VEntilator repair, and pulLOVEr design.

Name Calling (page 17)

If you can't bite, don't show your teeth.

Oddball of the Group
(page 18)

Figure D. It's the only set in which the intersection of the two parts does not reproduce the same shape as each of its figures.

Sudoku (page 19)

8	2	7	3	4	9	6	5	1
1	5	6	7	8	2	4	3	9
4	3	9	6	1	5	7	2	8
6	8	1	5	3	7	2	9	4
7	9	2	1	6	4	3	8	5
3	4	5	9	2	8	1	7	6
5	6	3	2	9	1	8	4	7
2	7	8	4	5	6	9	1	3
9	1	4	8	7	3	5	6	2

Arrow Web (page 19)

Use Some Sense
(pages 20–21)

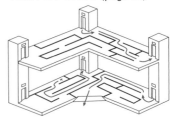

Vex-a-Gon (page 22)

Learned Crypto-quote
(page 22)

"I've never let my schooling interfere with my education."
—Mark Twain

You Are Here (page 23)

Word Ladder (page 24)

GONE, bone, bane, bare, barn, BORN

Number Crossword
(page 24)

3	6		
1	2	3	4
3	4	5	6
		8	8

Rhyme Time (page 25)

1. see me; 2. top cop; 3. fat bat; 4. chow now; 5. last cast or past cast; 6. pony crony; 7. Mars czars; 8. wrong thong; 9. coffee toffee; 10. sports reports

Word Columns (page 26)

"Logic takes care of itself; all we have to do is to look and see how it does it."   —Wittgenstein

Figure This Out in Your Own Good Time (page 26)

On a 24-hour clock

Hashi (page 27)

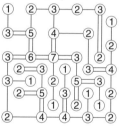

It's a Small Word, After All (page 28)

Say What? (page 29)

"A dirty joke is a sort of mental rebellion."

Fitting Words (page 29)

P	A	R	I	S
E	R	O	D	E
A	C	T	O	R
S	H	E	L	F

Crypto-group: European Cities (page 30)

NICE
LONDON
BARCELONA
VENICE
BERLIN

A Puzzling Perspective (page 30)

Undoubtedly

Girls' Names Letterbox (page 31)

Time for a Rhyme (pages 32–33)

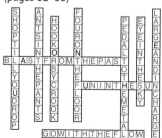

Answers

Twenty-four Jumble
(page 33)

$5 \times 4 + 4 = 24$

Fish Fantasy (page 34)

Word Ladder (page 35)

LOAN, loaf, leaf, lean, bean, beat, PEAT

Orderly Sequence (page 35)

The missing letter is O: These are the initial letters in the numbers one through nine.

1-2-3 (page 36)

Wacky Wordy (page 37)

Haste makes waste.

Sudoku (page 37)

1	2	3	8	7	4	5	6	9
5	6	7	9	3	2	1	8	4
8	4	9	6	5	1	2	3	7
9	1	6	2	4	7	8	5	3
3	5	8	1	9	6	4	7	2
4	7	2	3	8	5	9	1	6
2	9	1	7	6	8	3	4	5
6	8	5	4	2	3	7	9	1
7	3	4	5	1	9	6	2	8

Around the House
(pages 38–39)

At the Zoo (page 40)

ABCD Numbered (page 41)

	A	0	3	0	3	0	3
	B	0	2	1	2	1	3
	C	3	1	2	1	2	0
A B C D		3	0	3	0	3	0

0 3 0 3	D	B	D	B	D	B
3 0 3 0	C	A	C	A	C	A
0 2 2 2	D	C	B	C	D	B
3 1 1 1	C	A	D	A	B	A
0 3 2 1	D	B	C	B	C	B
3 0 1 2	C	A	D	A	D	A

Annual Sequence (page 41)

The missing letters are JY. The series represents the first and last letters of the months November through June.

Word Jigsaw (page 42)

```
M A D
A G A P E
T O T A L
  A R K
```

Shall We Dance? (page 43)

1. F. FOLK DANCE
2. D. BELLY DANCE
3. B. BREAKDANCE
4. E. SQUARE DANCE
5. A. FLAMENCO
6. C. TAP DANCE

The Yellow-Brick Road (page 44)

C. We can ask a liar, "Where doesn't the blue road start?"

Sudoku (page 44)

2	5	4	3	6	9	1	7	8
9	1	6	2	8	7	4	5	3
8	7	3	1	5	4	2	6	9
1	2	5	7	3	6	8	9	4
4	6	9	8	1	5	7	3	2
3	8	7	4	9	2	5	1	6
6	4	2	9	7	1	3	8	5
5	3	1	6	2	8	9	4	7
7	9	8	5	4	3	6	2	1

Uncrossed Paths (page 45)

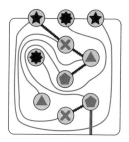

Name Calling (page 46)

Make sure to be in with your equals if you're going to fall out with your superiors.

Word Ladder (page 46)

PORCH, pouch, couch, cough, rough, ROUGE

Answers

Hashi (page 47)

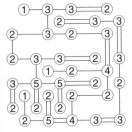

Movie Mania (page 48)

	Movie	Cinema	Star
1	Lord Sings	Premiere	Bud Pott
2	Gladys Hater	Worldwide	Ross Crawe
3	Forest Chump	Screenz	Owen McAllen
4	Atlantic 11	Olympic	Tim Panks

It's a Big Block (page 49)

There are 11 houses in the row.

A Puzzling Perspective
(page 49)

Unnecessary

Don't Miss the Boat On This One (page 50)

The number 1. The sum of each row is 20.

Anagram Heroes (page 50)

WOODY ALLEN

GEORGE LUCAS

STEVEN SPIELBERG

THOMAS EDISON

Thomas Edison was not a famous Hollywood director.

Cube Count (page 51)

There are 31 individual cubes.

Say What? (page 51)

"Education is an ornament in prosperity and a refuge in adversity."

Family Circle (page 52)

Leftover letters spell: marriage, dowry, culture

Quic-Kross (page 53)

RESERVED

Relations Problem
(page 53)

The relationship must be among these three possibilities:

1. Daughter-in-law; 2. wife's

aunt (wife's mother's brother's wife); 3. nephew's wife (wife's sister's son's wife).

Hat's Off (page 54)

1. Feather is different on top left hat; 2. zebra fabric on same hat; 3. buckle different on top right hat; 4. flower instead of feather pouf; 5. no rings on top of the cap; 6. second shelf on right longer; 7. brim different on hat with bow; 8. feather is white; 9. stand missing; 10. top of hat different; 11. no apostrophe in HATS; 12. triangle feathers going in opposite direction on bottom hat.

Calcu-doku (page 55)

2	4	3	1
4	1	2	3
3	2	1	4
1	3	4	2

Word Ladder (page 55)

BATTER, banter, barter, garter, garner, gurner, BURNER

Vex-a-Gon (page 56)

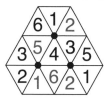

Made in the USA

(pages 56–57)

Name Calling (page 57)

The word is "figure."

Between the Lines
(page 58)

mammoth, man, manage; archipelago, architect, archive; forth, fortune, forty; ever, every, evict; owl, own, ox

"Every man is the architect of his own fortune."

Masyu (page 59)

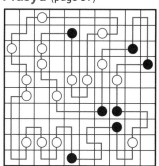

Answers

Hamster Treadmill
(page 60)

Device A

Cross-Math (page 61)

4	+	3	+	8	=	15
+		×		÷		
5	+	7	×	2	=	24
-		-		÷		
6	+	9	-	1	=	14
=		=		=		
3		12		4		

Picasso Pizza (Part II)
(page 62)

Figure B

Bird-Watching (page 62)

Across: eagle, emu, rook, swan, flamingo, hen, crow, gull, heron

Down: jay, hornbill, dove, owl, pheasant, tit, duck, hawk, lark

1-2-3 (page 63)

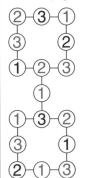

Tidy Up the Anagrams
(page 63)

standup and dustpan

Find the Word (page 64)

RusSO, FAther of two and a calypSO FAn, went to see the bosS OF A small coffee shop for a job. The boss, a friendly fellow, had Russo fix an espresSO FAst without making a mesS OF Anything. Russo twisted his torSO FAr away from the hot flame and cooked a miso-flavored espresSO FAster than anyone the boss had ever seen. The boss, an alleged MafioSO FAbled for his temper, loved the miso espresSO FAr more than he expected. InSOFAr as Russo's chance of a job, the bosS OF Another coffee shop alSO FAvored miso, and his offer was far more. RusSO FAred well and danced a calypSO FAncifully for his favorite customers.

A Puzzling Perspective
(page 64)

Wonderfully

Odd-Even Logidoku
(page 65)

Fists Are Flying
(pages 66–67)

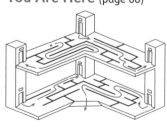

You Are Here (page 68)

Hashi (page 69)

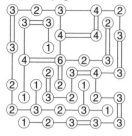

Word Ladder (page 69)

STOOL, spool, spoor, spoon, swoon, SWOOP

Puzzle Pieces (page 70)

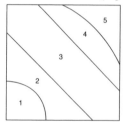

Short Sequence (page 70)

The letter J. This sequence represents planets Mercury, Venus, Earth, Mars, Jupiter, Saturn, Uranus, and Neptune.

Vex-a-Gon (page 71)

Answers

Name Calling (page 71)

Morsels

Caroline's Word Search
(pages 72–73)

Leftover letters spell: barometer, beverages, elaborate, paralegal

Homonyms (page 73)

Loot and lute

Word Jigsaw (page 74)

```
R E V
A R I A S
W R E S T
    W H Y
```

Sudoku (page 74)

8	1	4	3	6	9	5	2	7
2	6	9	4	7	5	3	1	8
7	3	5	2	8	1	4	6	9
4	5	2	8	1	7	9	3	6
3	9	7	6	2	4	1	8	5
1	8	6	9	5	3	2	7	4
5	7	3	1	9	6	8	4	2
9	4	8	7	3	2	6	5	1
6	2	1	5	4	8	7	9	3

Legion of L's (page 75)

1. lady; 2. lamppost; 3. layer cake; 4. leaves; 5. legs; 6. lemon; 7. lemonade; 8. life jacket; 9. light; 10. links; 11. lion; 12. loafers

Mondrian-esque (page 76)

There are 17 total squares.

8: 1 × 1

5: 2 × 2

4: 3 × 3

Wacky Wordy (page 76)

Have ("halve") a nice day.

Blind Ambition (page 77)

"I always wanted to be somebody, but now I realize I should have been more specific."
—Lily Tomlin

Odd One Out (page 77)

COW. All the other words can be used as nouns (other than birds or mammals).

Quic-Kross (page 78)

PRATFALL

Calcu-doku (page 78)

1	3	4	5	2
5	2	1	4	3
4	1	2	3	5
2	5	3	1	4
3	4	5	2	1

Music Letterbox (page 79)

1	2	3	4	5	6	7	8	9	10	11	12	13
G	H	P	I	A	N	O	J	W	T	X	K	F

14	15	16	17	18	19	20	21	22	23	24	25	26
D	R	U	M	Z	L	S	B	E	C	V	Y	Q

Triple-Jointed (pages 80–81)

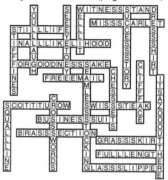

Logic-cadabra! (page 82)

Marvella is wearing a green headband. Ann says she does not know what color her headband is. She would know only if Beth and Marvella were both wearing yellow headbands, which would mean she was wearing green. Because she can't tell, Beth and Marvella are either both wearing green, or one is wearing green and the other yellow. Beth hears what Ann has said and knows she and Marvella are either both wearing green, or one is wearing green and the other yellow. If Marvella's eyes are covered by a yellow headband, Beth would know she's wearing green. Since Beth said she doesn't know her color, that means Marvella is wearing green.

Answers

Try Saying This Three Times Really Fast
(page 82)

Wednesday

Remember Me? (Part II)
(page 84)

Flames, Gargoyle, Hot Dog, Balloons, Acorns, Scarecrow, Decoy

Hitori (page 84)

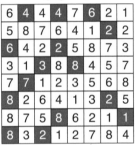

Let It Shine by Alpha Sleuth™ (page 85)

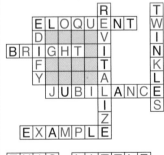

Revolutionary Event
(page 86)

BOWS - W + TWO - W + N + TIE - I + CAP - C + DART - D + Y = BOSTON TEA PARTY

Sudoku (page 87)

6	4	1	5	3	8	9	2	7
7	8	3	2	9	4	5	6	1
2	9	5	1	7	6	4	8	3
5	6	7	9	4	3	8	1	2
3	1	4	8	2	7	6	9	5
9	2	8	6	5	1	7	3	4
1	5	2	4	8	9	3	7	6
4	7	9	3	6	2	1	5	8
8	3	6	7	1	5	2	4	9

Sucker Bet (page 87)

Shirley has been married twice to guys named Vern, and she has visited Atlantic City once with each of them. Shirley is the second Vern's first and only wife.

On Your Head (page 88)

Cube Quandary (page 89)

The length is 6 times the height and 3 times the width.

A President's Creed
(page 89)

"When I do good, I feel good. When I do bad, I feel bad. That's my religion."
—Abraham Lincoln

Number Crossword
(page 90)

3	3		1	6
6	5	4	3	2
	2	2	5	
9	5	3	7	1
1	3		9	7

Rhyme Time (page 91)

1. Gates skates; 2. Blass class; 3. worry Murray; 4. Haley's dailies; 5. Clinton hintin'

Theme: These are famous people named Bill.

School Correction
(page 92)

	Action	Object	Tool
1	wash	floor	brush
2	clean	shed	roller
3	sweep	path	cloth
4	paint	car	mop

Who's Watching? (page 93)

It was 8 pm. As the faster watch gained on the slower one by 3 minutes per hour, it was exactly 1 hour ahead after 20 hours (20 × 3 = 60).

Vex-a-Gon (page 93)

Missing Connections
(page 94)

Arrow Web (page 95)

Upside Down and Backward (page 95)

NOON

Say What? (page 96)

"Love so amazing, so divine, demands my soul, my life, my all."

What a Racket (page 96)

The letter M, as in the tennis terms "Game, Set, Match."

Perfect Score (page 97)

3 + 40 + 57 = 100

Word Ladder (page 97)

TRUCK, trick, crick, click, slick, slack, SNACK

Elevator Words (page 98)

1. Falls Church; 2. church bench; 3. bench press; 4. press pass; 5. pass key; 6. key card; 7. card game

Twenty-four Jumble (page 99)

9 - 5 × 6 = 24

Liar's Logic (page 99)

The liars are A and D. Because A is a liar, C is a truth-teller; therefore D is a liar, and B is right when he says that C tells the truth.

Get It Straight (page 100)

Sudoku (page 101)

3	5	1	7	8	9	2	6	4
4	2	7	6	3	5	8	9	1
6	9	8	1	4	2	7	3	5
2	7	4	9	6	3	5	1	8
9	3	5	4	1	8	6	7	2
1	8	6	5	2	7	9	4	3
5	4	9	8	7	1	3	2	6
7	6	2	3	5	4	1	8	9
8	1	3	2	9	6	4	5	7

Anagram Snack (page 101)

spectrum and crumpets

Rhyme Time (page 102)

1. one gun; 2. numb thumb; 3. monk shrunk; 4. Hubble trouble; 5. levity brevity

Cross-Math (page 103)

9	+	3	+	5	=	17
×		÷		+		
2	÷	1	+	6	=	8
-		+		+		
8	×	4	-	7	=	25
=		=		=		
10		7		18		

Word Jumble (page 103)

Personality

Crypto-botany (page 104)

Tomato (name of plant). There are more varieties of tomatoes than of any other vegetable. Originally, Europeans thought tomatoes were poisonous and grew them as ornamental plants. They were grown by Thomas Jefferson in 1781, but weren't known as an edible food until 1834. Tomatoes have also been called garden apple, gold apple, and love apple.

Masyu (page 105)

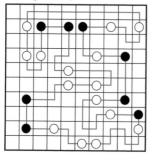

Fitting Words (page 106)

Get in Shape (page 107)

Figure D cannot be reassembled from Figure 1 by cutting it into two pieces.

Rich Riddle (page 107)

$387,420,489. Johnny could have thought of 9 to the 9th power, or 387,420,489.

Word Ladder (page 108)

SMILE, smite, spite, spire, hire, shirt, short, shore, CHORE

Odd One Out (page 108)

RIGHT. The other words sound like one of the 5 human senses.

ABCD (page 109)

A	2	2	1	1	1	2
B	2	0	2	2	2	1
C	2	1	1	0	3	2

A	B	C	D						
				0	3	2	3	0	1
2	1	1	2	A	D	B	D	C	A
2	1	2	1	C	A	D	B	A	C
1	2	2	1	B	D	C	A	C	B
1	2	2	1	C	A	B	D	B	C
2	1	2	1	A	C	D	B	C	A
1	2	0	3	B	D	A	D	B	D

1-2-3 (page 109)

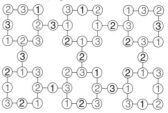

Acrostic (pages 110–111)

A. Henry Ford; B. gravitates;
C. peeves; D. immense;
E. hemming; F. hoof;
G. Aberdeen; H. minstrel;
I. ointment; J. plotting.

"Time and money spent in helping men to do more for themselves is far better than mere giving."

Answers

Hitori (page 111)

8	3	1	7	2	6	**8**	5
1	1	**1**	8	3	7	2	4
6	**7**	7	**7**	4	3	**3**	8
7	5	3	2	1	**7**	4	6
1	4	5	3	6	2	7	**5**
4	7	6	5	**2**	8	3	2
8	6	4	**7**	8	1	**2**	3
3	2	**2**	1	5	4	6	**3**

Break the Code (page 112)

Star = 5, Diamond = 3,
Circle = 2, and Arrow = 1

The diagonal sum is 9.

Cast-a-Word (page 112)

1. A B S U V Z
2. C D I J L W
3. E H K M T Y
4. G N O P R X

Hamster Treadmill
(page 113)

Device A

Word Jigsaw (page 114)

Think Twice (page 114)

The number 11. Starting with
166, divide each number by
2 and add 3 to get the next
number in the sequence.

Cube Quandary (page 115)

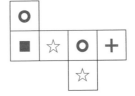

Hurry! (pages 116–117)

Name Calling (page 118)

Receding

A Puzzling Perspective
(page 118)

Foreclosure

Anagram Rhyme (page 119)

fork handles/four candles

Mixed Figures (Part II)
(page 120)

The triangle appeared twice.

Exercise Time (page 120)

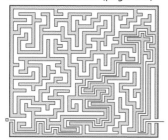

Vex-a-Gon (page 121)

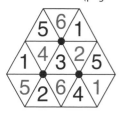

Odd-Even Logidoku
(page 121)

7	6	2	8	1	5	3	4	9
9	8	4	2	3	6	7	1	5
1	3	5	9	4	7	2	8	6
2	5	8	1	7	3	6	9	4
3	9	1	4	6	2	8	5	7
4	7	6	5	8	9	1	2	3
5	2	7	3	9	1	4	6	8
6	4	9	7	2	8	5	3	1
8	1	3	6	5	4	9	7	2

Star Power (page 122)

Say What? (page 123)

"All happy families resemble one another, each unhappy family is unhappy in its own way."

Liar's Logic (page 123)

The liars are A and C. If A were telling the truth, B would have to be lying, making D and E liars as well (which is too many liars). The process of elimination leads to the answer that B, D, and E are telling the truth.

Cross Count (page 124)

²t	⁹r	⁵e	¹s	17
⁵w	¹a	⁹i	²t	17
¹a	³c	⁹r	⁵e	18
¹s	⁵e	⁵e	⁴m	15
9	18	28	12	

Answers

Kingdom of K's (page 125)

1. kangaroo; 2. kayak; 3. kerchief;
4. keystone; 5. kite; 6. knapsack;
7. knife; 8. knitting; 9. knitting
needles; 10. knot; 11. knuckles

Ball Games (pages 126–127)

Hashi (page 128)

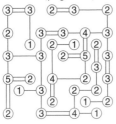

Fitting Words (page 129)

F	I	R	S	T
I	R	A	T	E
J	O	K	E	S
I	N	E	P	T

Between the Lines
(page 130)

inactive, inalienable, inane;
rig, right, rigid; hum, human,
humble; theme, themselves,
then; invasion, invent, inverse

"Human beings have an
inalienable right to invent
themselves."

Calcu-doku (page 131)

3	2	5	4	1
2	5	1	3	4
4	3	2	1	5
1	4	3	5	2
5	1	4	2	3

Word Ladder (page 131)

JACKET, packet, picket, wicket,
wicker, wicked, LICKED

Name that Scramblegram (page 132)

	G	R	E	A	T	A	R	M	
	M	A	R	G	A	R	E	T	
R	C							S	S
E	A							A	A
A	R							M	T
L	O							A	A
C	L							N	N
O	I							T	H
I	N							H	A
N	E							A	M
	K	A	T	H	L	E	E	N	
	T	H	E	A	N	K	L	E	

A	E	C	R	I	H	T	E	N
C	A	T	H	E	R	I	N	E

World Cities Letterbox
(page 133)

1	2	3	4	5	6	7	8	9	10	11	12	13
H	J	O	C	P	A	R	I	S	D	V	F	K

14	15	16	17	18	19	20	21	22	23	24	25	26
Q	Y	N	Z	E	U	T	B	X	M	G	W	L

264

Start Your Day by Alpha Sleuth™ (page 134)

RISE AND SHINE

For Heavenly Navigators, a Star Maze
(page 135)

Perfect Score (page 136)

4 + 4 + 92 = 100

Word Ladder (page 136)

GLOSS, glass, grass, crass, class, CLASP

Cross-Math (page 137)

4	+	8	-	1	=	11
+		÷		+		
6	+	2	+	7	=	15
-		+		+		
9	+	5	-	3	=	11
=		=		=		
1		9		11		

Whistling Workers
(page 137)

The letter B. These are the Seven Dwarfs: Doc, Grumpy, Happy, Sneezy, Bashful, Sleepy, and Dopey.

Hangin' 10 (pages 138–139)

```
D U D E Y O U J S H P D R O U
D E X A L E X A A L I D E K N
D R E V I U Q O W K P T V C H
U A A T A A C S S W E L L T K
C D K I R I P C U R L G I C K
K I D I P A I V K C T S S A U
D C A E N S L F A D N U K N U
A A D R K E F U G L E O I E F
I V L O B R O D E B O S E U T
E R H R G H T U T U D P Q G A
N D A N A S Q S D C T I E N U
I B I L L A B O N G H W V A E
M O O R N E E R G R I S A H K
G M C O Y L R A N G L L E C T
E B U T I O N O F S T I C K S
```

Leftover letters spell: Dude! You should know that a stick is a surfboard and a quiver is a collection of sticks!

Answers

Quic-Kross (page 139)

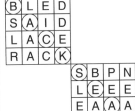

BACKSEAT

Number Maze (page 140)

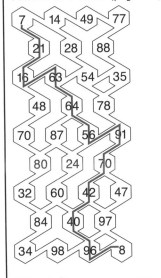

Word Jigsaw (page 141)

Digital Sudoku (page 141)

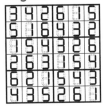

Trifling Truffles (page 142)

Astra's truffle box contained
1 maple, 3 cherry, 1 vanilla, and
3 fudge.

Bunny's truffle box contained
1 maple, 4 cherry, 2 vanilla, and
1 fudge.

Coco's truffle box contained
1 maple, 1 cherry, 3 vanilla, and
3 fudge.

Danielle's truffle box contained
2 maple, 1 cherry, 3 vanilla, and
2 fudge.

Evie's truffle box contained
5 maple, 1 cherry, 1 vanilla, and
1 fudge.

Hashi (page 143)

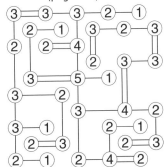

Star Power (page 144)

The Whys and Wherefores (page 145)

The value of Y could be anywhere between 2 and 6.

Beautiful Words (page 146)

MELODY, GOSSAMER, TRANQUIL, MURMURING, ORIOLE

Name Calling (page 146)

"Push" and "Pull" are written on the door of success.

Cube Quandary (page 147)

Cube C is incorrect.

Cube F looks like this:

Find the Word (page 148)

Nice T, RAPper extraordinaire, rapped aT RAPid-fire speeds

for his rapt fans. ApT RAPper Master Apple toured with Nice T, RAPping and filling in as an exTRA Person in the band. At a concert, T accidentally ran into the orchesTRA Pit and Master Apple became a hiT RAPping in his place. Nice T repeated his manTRA, "Please Let Me Rap" and returned as an ulTRA Performer, topping the charts again and trampling Apple in his wake. Apple goT RAPiers and challenged T to a rapper duel, but T apologized and Apple and T RAPidly became friends and dueT RAPpers again.

Cross Count (page 148)

⁷p	⁵e	¹a	13
⁸h	¹a	¹s	10
⁹i	⁹r	²k	20
24	15	4	

Famous Address (page 149)

"Four score and seven years ago..."

Read Between the Lines (page 149)

Figure C is next, because if you ignore the changing dots, you'll see that the figures contain the letters in the word NEWS.

Answers

Mondrianize It! (page 150)

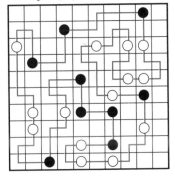

Figure This Out (page 151)

Figure A is different.

Memory Test with a Twist (Part II) (page 152)

The straight memory part of this puzzle is of medium difficulty, but finding what the words have in common is tough: Each word contains a consecutive 3-letter alphabet sequence, such as ABC in CRABCAKE, DEF in INDEFINITE, and so on.

The words from page 151 are CALMNESS, SOMNOLENT, LAUGHING, AFGHANISTAN, and ASTUTE.

Go Figure (page 152)

						144
2	3	4	1	3	4	288
3	2	1	6	1	2	72
6	5	2	3	2	4	1440
2	3	6	2	5	1	360
4	1	2	3	6	3	432
2	6	4	4	3	4	2304

576 540 384 432 543 384 384

Masyu (page 153)

Help Find Our Missing Circus Acts! (page 154)

Stilt Walker, Aerial Acrobatics, Sword Swallower, Human Cannonball, Trapeze Artist, Magic Act, Music Performers, Bareback Rider, Fortune Teller. The missing letters spell Lion Tamer.

Oddball of the Group
(page 155)

Figure 4, because it's the only figure that doesn't have an unconnected single straight line in its configuration.

Word Ladder (page 155)

PUNCH, bunch, bench, beach, peach, PEACE

That's a Hot One
(pages 156–157)

Number Crossword
(page 158)

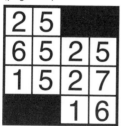

Wacky Wordy (page 158)

Tomatoes (tom 8 O's)

More Fun than a Barrel of Grapes (page 159)

Elevator Words (page 160)

1. ice cream; 2. cream cheese;
3. cheese press; 4. press box;
5. box camera; 6. camera ready;
7. ready made

Odd-Even Logidoku
(page 161)

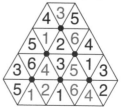

Vex-a-Gon (page 161)

Answers

Hashi (page 162)

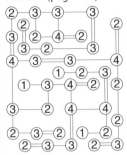

Name Calling (page 163)

A guest is like the rain: When he persists, he is a nuisance.

A Puzzling Perspective
(page 163)

Expectorate

Word Columns (page 164)

Scotty: "She's all yours, sir. All systems automated and ready. A chimpanzee and two trainees could run her!" Kirk: "Thank you, Mr. Scott, I'll try not to take that personally." (*Star Trek*)

1-2-3 (page 165)

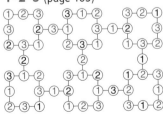

Fitting Words (page 165)

Find It (pages 166–167)

Blue: navy, indigo, sapphire;
Round: coin, ring, yo-yo;
Baseball: bat, pitcher, umpire;
Movies: *Tootsie, Toys, Twister;*
Capitals: Austin, Boston, Salem.

Sequencing (page 167)

640. It is the 4 times table (4, 8, 12, 16, 20, 24, 28, 32, 36, 40) split into sets of 3 numbers.

Orbiting Orbs (page 168)

Code-doku (page 169)

M	N	U	O	L	V	R	E	G
L	O	G	R	E	M	U	V	N
V	E	R	G	U	N	O	M	L
N	R	M	E	G	L	V	O	U
U	V	L	N	O	R	E	G	M
E	G	O	V	M	U	L	N	R
R	M	N	L	V	E	G	U	O
G	U	E	M	R	O	N	L	V
O	L	V	U	N	G	M	R	E

MR. GREEN, REVOLVER, LOUNGE

It's a Song (page 169)

"One for the money, two for the show..."

Kakuro (page 170)

Perfect Score (page 171)

7 + 23 + 70 = 100

Word Ladder (page 171)

HILL, hilt, halt, halo, hall, gall, gale, PALE

Digital Sudoku (page 172)

Rhyme Time (page 173)

1. wind kind; 2. hard yard;
3. warm dorm; 4. tram scam;
5. pork fork; 6. rare chair; 7. regal eagle; 8. sweet treat; 9. troupe group; 10. groovy movie;
11. dental rental; 12. skeeter meter

The Upper Crust by Alpha Sleuth™ (page 174)

LIVING LARGE

Vex-a-Gon (page 175)

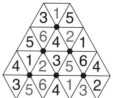

Cast-a-Word (page 175)

1. A B K N P R
2. C L U V W X
3. D I M O T Z
4. E F G H S Y

Hitori (page 176)

2	2	2	4	5	7	3	3
2	7	6	6	1	8	2	3
1	5	8	2	4	3	7	4
5	1	3	4	4	6	2	8
6	3	2	7	4	4	5	7
8	4	6	1	3	8	6	5
4	2	5	6	3	1	1	7
3	6	5	8	7	5	4	1

Star Power (page 177)

		2	8	5	3	8	
	5	7	4	★	1	★	2
	6	★	3	6	7	6	4
5	1	8	2	■	8	★	1
7	★	4	■	1	2	5	3
6	2	3	5	8	★	7	
5	★	7	★	4	3	6	
8	4	1	2	6			

Eavesdropping Logic
(page 178)

The answer is D, as every other option entails a misreading (or an over-reading) of the situation. We cannot conclude that Simone dislikes someone just because she is annoyed, or that Matthew has "other" concerns when they are

"related" ones. And just because Simone misinterprets Matthew on this occasion doesn't mean she is generally a bad judge of character.

Go Figure (page 178)

20

2	4	5	3	2	240
1	3	3	5	5	225
2	3	1	4	4	96
3	2	5	4	1	120
1	3	4	2	2	48

12 216 300 480 80   48

At the Movies (page 179)

1. Each wears glasses; 2. they have their eyes shut; 3. they are wearing polo shirts; 4. have large boxes of popcorn; 5. right hands are to their mouths; 6. each has a drink; 7. all have feet up on backs of seats; 8. they are all women.

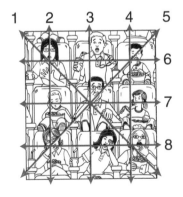

ABCD (page 180)

	A	1	2	1	3	0	2
	B	2	2	2	0	2	1
	C	3	0	1	2	2	1
A B C D	D	0	2	2	1	2	2

3	1	1	1	A	B	A	C	D	A
2	0	2	2	C	A	D	A	C	D
0	3	1	2	B	D	B	D	B	C
3	0	2	1	C	A	D	A	C	A
0	3	1	2	B	D	B	C	B	D
1	2	2	1	C	B	C	A	D	B

You Are Here (page 181)

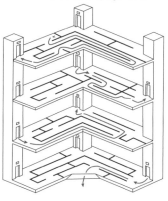

Logidoku (page 182)

3	2	9	5	8	7	1	6	4
1	8	4	2	3	6	5	9	7
7	6	5	1	4	9	8	2	3
8	4	3	9	6	5	7	1	2
5	7	2	3	1	8	6	4	9
6	9	1	7	2	4	3	8	5
9	5	6	4	7	1	2	3	8
4	3	8	6	5	2	9	7	1
2	1	7	8	9	3	4	5	6

Missing Someone?
(page 182)

Answer C is correct. The sum of each pair of numbers is 31.

Cube Quandary (page 183)

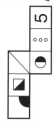

Cheap Tickets
(pages 184–185)

Crypto-Logic (page 186)

DISGUISED. The numbers that repeat are two 7s, two 3s, and two 2s. These total 24. Q is therefore worth 10; S is worth 2; D is worth 7. This means that E = 14 - 10, or 4. The remaining unidentified repeated number is 3, so I is 3. Therefore G is 9 and U is 1.

Animal Sounds (page 186)

H80. Substitute each "80" for "AT" to get BAT, CAT, GOAT, HAT, RAT, and STOAT. Obviously HAT is the only one that's not a bird or mammal

Cross-Math (page 187)

5	+	9	-	8	=	6
+		-		+		
2	×	4	-	6	=	2
+		+		÷		
3	÷	1	+	7	=	10
=		=		=		
10		6		2		

Between the Lines
(page 188)

entertain, enthusiasm, entice; ache, achieve, Achilles; grease, great, greed; note, nothing, notice

"Nothing great was ever achieved without enthusiasm."

Name Calling (page 189)

When luck joins in the game, cleverness scores double.

Name Game (Part II)
(page 190)

1. Angela/Jamie; 2. Jonathan/Stephanie; 3. Georgina/Howard; 4. Davina/Robert; 5. Tom/Dorothy; 6. Carol/Gordon; 7. Matthew/Jane; 8. Peter/Caroline; 9. Heather/David

Vex-a-Gon (page 190)

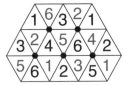

Hashi (page 191)

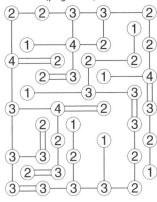

Logidoku (page 192)

3	2	8	9	6	5	1	4	7
7	9	6	3	1	4	5	2	8
1	5	4	7	2	8	6	3	9
6	4	1	2	3	9	7	8	5
8	3	9	6	5	7	4	1	2
2	7	5	8	4	1	9	6	3
5	6	3	4	7	2	8	9	1
9	1	2	5	8	6	3	7	4
4	8	7	1	9	3	2	5	6

Eleven Coins (page 192)

Put 3 coins in each pan. If they balance, all are true coins and you can put 5 of them against the 5 not used to see which is heaviest. If there is not a balance from the first weighing, the 5 unused coins are true. Balance 3 of these against the heavier group of 3 coins from the first weighing to determine if the fake is heavier or lighter than a true coin.

Cross Count (page 193)

R ₉	O ₆	B ₂	E ₅	22
E ₅	V ₄	I ₉	L ₃	21
S ₁	E ₅	T ₂	S ₁	9
T ₂	R ₉	E ₅	E ₅	21
17	24	18	14	

Rhyme Time (page 193)

1. drill skill; 2. reach beach;
3. faulted malted; 4. pester jester;
5. reoccupation preoccupation

Word Columns (page 194)

"If an article is attractive, or useful, or inexpensive, they'll stop making it tomorrow; if it's all three, they stopped making it yesterday."

—Mignon McLaughlin

How Many Rectangles?
(page 194)

There are 34 rectangles in all: 2 rectangles are 4×2; 4 rectangles are 3×2; 4 rectangles are 4×1; 16 rectangles are 2×1, and 8 rectangles are 3×1.

Word Ladder (page 195)

FOLKY, folly, holly, holey, honey, money, MONET

Digital Sudoku (page 195)

For Intrepid Hikers
(page 196)

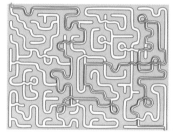

Kakuro (page 197)

		16	10			15	17	
	16	9	7		12	3	9	16
	9	7	2	14 29	9	7	8	5	9
	11		1	3	2	5	11	2	1
4	6		1	3	24 9	7	9	8
6	3	1	2	4 9	3	1		
3	1	2	12 10	1	2	3	4	16
	10	3	1	2	4	17	2	7
3	23	15	8	7	18 13	1	3	9
13	1	9	3	24 17	8	9		
8	2	6	29 5	8	9	7	5	16
	19	8	3	7	1	17	8	9
		11	2	9	16	9	7	

Answers

Cast-a-Word (page 198)

1. A F H M R T
2. B G J O S Y
3. C I L N U V
4. D E K P Q W

Classical Sequence
(page 198)

E—these are the opening notes
of Beethoven's Fifth Symphony)

Grid Fill (page 199)

A	M	O	U	N	T
D	A	N	C	E	S
D	A	R	W	I	N
S	U	G	A	R	S
M	O	N	D	A	Y
K	E	T	T	L	E
S	P	R	A	L	L

Greenback Ovals
(page 200)

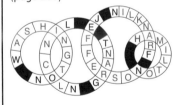

Movie Title and Director
Cryptogram (page 201)

1. *North by Northwest:* Alfred
   Hitchcock
2. *The Shining:* Stanley Kubrick
3. *Citizen Kane:* Orson Welles
4. *Raging Bull:* Martin Scorsese

1-2-3 (page 202)

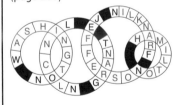

Sudoku (page 202)

6	2	1	8	5	7	4	9	3
3	4	9	2	6	1	5	7	8
5	7	8	3	4	9	6	2	1
8	9	2	7	3	6	1	5	4
7	1	6	5	9	4	3	8	2
4	3	5	1	8	2	9	6	7
2	6	3	9	1	8	7	4	5
1	8	4	6	7	5	2	3	9
9	5	7	4	2	3	8	1	6

Rating the Guys (page 203)

Antonio is a 12. The dating
service rates each guy by giving
him 3 points for every syllable in
his name.

Fitting Words (page 203)

J	A	C	K	S
A	R	E	N	A
M	I	L	E	S
B	A	L	E	S

As a Formality
(pages 204–205)

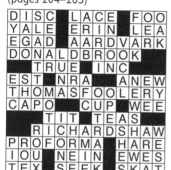

D	I	S	C		L	A	C	E		F	O	O
Y	A	L	E		E	R	I	N		L	E	A
E	G	A	D		A	A	R	D	V	A	R	K
D	O	N	A	L	D	B	R	O	O	K
		T	R	U	E		I	N	C
E	S	T		N	R	A		A	N	E	W
T	H	O	M	A	S	F	O	O	L	E	R	Y
C	A	P	O		C	U	P		W	E	E
		T	I	T		T	E	A	S
	R	I	C	H	A	R	D	S	H	A	W
P	R	O	F	O	R	M	A		H	A	R	E
I	O	U		N	E	I	N		E	W	E	S
T	E	X		S	E	E	K		S	K	A	T

Lunch Plans (page 206)

2,519 guests were invited.

2,519/3 = 839 tables + 2 guests left over

2,519/5 = 503 + 4 guests over

2,519/7 = 359 + 6 guests over

2,519/9 = 279 + 8 guests over

2,519/11 = 229 tables; all seated

Word Ladder (page 206)

CLOUD, clout, flout, float, gloat, groat, GREAT

Perfect Score (page 207)

47 + 38 + 15 = 100

Clone It! (page 208)

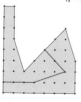

Between the Lines
(page 209)

Coupon, courage, course; battery, battle, bawl; hale, half, hall; Dane, danger, dangle

"Courage in danger is half the battle."

Logidoku (page 210)

5	9	8	7	1	6	4	2	3
7	6	4	3	8	2	9	1	5
2	3	1	9	4	5	6	8	7
9	7	5	8	6	4	1	3	2
3	8	6	2	7	1	5	4	9
1	4	2	5	9	3	8	7	6
6	1	9	4	3	7	2	5	8
4	2	7	6	5	8	3	9	1
8	5	3	1	2	9	7	6	4

Wacky Wordy (page 210)

One-hit wonder (one "hit," one "der")

Alien Mutations (page 211)

A to body circle, B head circle, C add the antennae, D remove the antennae, E to biped, F body square, G remove rear appendages, H head circle, I head square, J remove front appendages, K add rear appendage, L to biped, M to quadruped, N to biped, O add front appendages, P body circle

Paint-by-Number
(page 212)

Lou painted 6 yards more than Bud.

If the length of the street is L yards, Lou painted L - 3 + 6 yards, which equals L + 3 yards. Bud painted 3 + L - 6 yards, which equals L - 3 yards.

Therefore, Lou painted 6 yards more than Bud. The length of the street is irrelevant.

Vex-a-Gon (page 212)

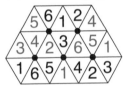

Identity Parade (page 213)

A   B   C   D

Word Ladder (page 214)

Answers may vary. FISH, wish, wise, wine, wink, wonk, honk, HOOK

Cross-Math (page 214)

5	+	6	-	3	=	8
÷		+		+		
1	×	8	÷	4	=	2
-		-		+		
2	×	7	-	9	=	5
=		=		=		
3		7		16		

ABCD (page 215)

A	C	D	C	D	C	D	C	A
B	A	B	D	B	A	B	D	B
D	B	C	B	C	B	C	B	D
B	A	D	A	D	C	A	C	A
A	B	A	C	A	D	B	A	C
B	A	D	B	D	B	D	B	D

Fit It (pages 216–217)

C	O	S	T	A	R		C	A	C	H	E	D
O	R	I	O	L	E		A	L	P	I	N	E
D	A	R	T	E	D		S	L	U	R	P	S
E	T	E		O	N	T	O		E	L	I	
S	E	D	A	N		B	A	T		O	A	R
			R	O	M	A	N		T	U	N	E
M	O	R	T	G	A	G	E	R	A	T	E	S
O	R	E	S		T	A	T	E	R			
R	I	P		A	T	M		P	E	S	O	S
A	G	O		B	R	E	W			T	I	C
L	A	S	S	I	E		A	T	T	I	L	A
E	M	E	N	D	S		S	E	A	L	E	D
S	I	D	L	E	S		P	A	P	E	R	S

Common Sense (page 217)

The letter H. These are the 5 senses: sight, smell, hearing, touch, and taste.

Elevator Words (page 218)

1. pitch pipe; 2. pipe dream;
3. dream team; 4. team spirit;
5. spirit gum; 6. gum arabic;
7. Arabic numeral

Say What? (page 219)

"It was high counsel that I had
once heard given to a young
person, 'Always do what you are
afraid to do.'"

Courier Confusion (Part II) (page 220)

Don Jensen,
The Willows,
4th Floor,
94 Grand Oaks Avenue,
Bakersfield,
Connecticut,
CA 10016

Star Power (page 220)

7	3	2	6	5	6	1
5	★	1	★	7	★	4
8	6	4	3	8	2	3
3	★	7	★	6	★	5
2	1	5	2	1	7	4
6	★	4	★	8	★	3
8	3	7	3	6	2	5

Digital Sudoku (page 221)

6	3	2	1	4	5
1	5	4	3	6	2
4	2	5	6	3	1
3	6	1	5	2	4
5	4	3	2	1	6
2	1	6	4	5	3

A Shapely Challenge (page 221)

There are 41 quadrilaterals.

Won't You Join Us?

(pages 222–223)

The newly formed words are:
arrowhead, background, bagpipe,
bandwagon, barnstorm, bedtime,
blockbuster, bookmobile,
breakfast, brickbat, buckskin,
bulldog, butterfly, catbird,
clockwork, cornerstone, eyebrow,
featherweight, flowerpot,
ladybug, nailfile, newsstand,
pigtail, sandbox, thumbtack

Class Schedule (page 224)

	Subject	Teacher	Room
1	Geography	Irving	E9
2	Art	Harrison	A2
3	Chemistry	Jones	F7
4	English	Kettering	D5
5	Biology	Lee	C8
6	History	Gates	B1

Answers

Codeword (page 225)

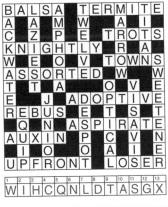

Fences (page 226)

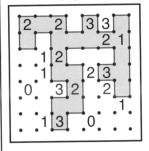

Concise Concept (page 226)

Figure 5, because it's a concave shape; all of the other figures are convex shapes.

Kakuro (page 227)

	22	24				3	23	13
16	9	7				3	2	1
6	2	1	3		6	2	1	3
25	8	9	7	1	29	8	5	9	7
8	3	5	20	9	7	4	10	8	2
		3	2	1	19	9	5	2	3
	16		7	9		3	1
	24	7	8	9	15	
3	2	1	15	7	8	30
17	9	8	7	16	7	9
13	7	6	19	7	9	3	15	8	7
28	9	8	7	4	23	1	9	5	8
8	1	5	2		18	8	1	6
15	8	7			16	7	9

Crypto-Logic (page 228)

Concealed

Go Figure (page 228)

							864
2	3	4	4	2	5	1	960
4	2	5	1	1	3	4	480
3	1	3	2	2	4	3	432
3	4	2	6	4	1	2	1152
2	3	4	3	3	3	5	3240
5	2	3	4	1	2	3	720
3	6	2	1	4	3	2	864

2160 864 2880 576 192 1080 720   864

Number Crossword (page 229)

		8	2
1	4	1	4
1	8	9	8
1	4		

Vex-a-Gon (page 229)

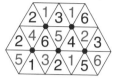

Supermarket Shenanigans (page 230)

Checkout Charlie bought a doughnut and a carton of eggnog. The applesauce cost $2.10, the pound of beef cost $3.30, the bag of candy cost $1.90, the doughnut cost $1.00, and the carton of eggnog cost $3.80.

Logidoku (page 231)

7	9	2	3	5	1	6	8	4
5	6	1	9	4	8	7	2	3
3	4	8	2	7	6	5	1	9
4	8	6	5	1	7	9	3	2
1	2	7	8	3	9	4	5	6
9	3	5	6	2	4	1	7	8
6	7	9	1	8	3	2	4	5
2	1	3	4	6	5	8	9	7
8	5	4	7	9	2	3	6	1

Pharmacy Fountain (page 232)

Hashi (page 233)

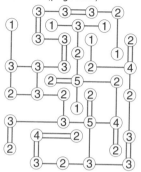

Mathematics Letterbox (page 234)

1	2	3	4	5	6	7	8	9	10	11	12	13
J	C	Y	B	Q	H	Z	K	U	W	M	X	O

14	15	16	17	18	19	20	21	22	23	24	25	26
P	S	V	T	R	I	A	N	G	L	E	F	D

Cross Sums (page 235)

		1433				
		431	439	386		
	76	121	177	98	64	
3	11	57	43	47	6	4
	5	10	30	2	7	
		12	1	8		
			9			

Flip the Cards (page 236)

The answer is D. You don't have to turn all the 7s, because you just need to know that no other numbers have Fs on them, not that all 7s do.

Answers

Sudoku (page 236)

9	6	5	3	4	8	7	1	2
8	4	2	7	6	1	5	3	9
1	7	3	5	9	2	6	8	4
4	5	1	2	3	9	8	7	6
3	2	9	8	7	6	4	5	1
7	8	6	4	1	5	2	9	3
2	3	4	1	8	7	9	6	5
5	9	8	6	2	3	1	4	7
6	1	7	9	5	4	3	2	8

Sciences Scramblegram
(page 237)

O	S	M	C	O	O	Y	L	G
C	O	S	M	O	L	O	G	Y

1-2-3 (page 238)

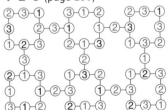

Word Jigsaw (page 239)

B	O	B		
Y	I	E	L	D
E	L	D	E	R
	S	T	Y	

Digital Sudoku (page 240)

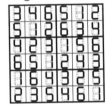

Fitting Words (page 240)

E	R	A	S	E
G	U	S	T	O
G	L	E	A	N
Y	E	A	R	S

Kakuro (page 241)

Shakespeare's Women
(pages 242–243)

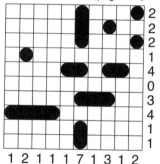

Leftover letters spell: Lady Northumberland

Battle Boats (page 244)

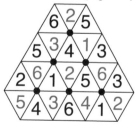

2
2
2
1
4
0
3
4
1
1

1 2 1 1 1 7 1 3 1 2

Coffee Break (page 244)

Note that 12 percent is the same as $\frac{3}{25}$. Fill the 5-cup mug and dissolve the coffee packet in the water. This liquid has a coffee concentration of 20 percent, or $\frac{1}{5}$. Pour 3 cups from the 5-cup mug into the 3-cup mug.

Discard the remaining 2 cups from the 5-cup mug. Pour the liquid from the 3-cup mug into the 5-cup mug. The 3 cups of liquid in the 5-cup mug contains $\frac{3}{5}$ of a cup of actual coffee. Fill the remainder of the 5-cup mug with water to dilute the liquid to a coffee concentration of $\frac{3}{5}$ of a cup out of 5 cups, or $\frac{3}{25}$, which is 12 percent.

Sudoku (page 245)

6	7	5	1	8	3	4	2	9
2	8	3	9	5	4	1	6	7
9	1	4	2	7	6	3	5	8
1	4	7	5	3	2	8	9	6
3	2	8	6	1	9	7	4	5
5	6	9	8	4	7	2	1	3
8	3	2	4	6	5	9	7	1
7	9	6	3	2	1	5	8	4
4	5	1	7	9	8	6	3	2

Vex-a-Gon (page 245)

Index

Index

Logic